The Art of Success
and
In the Ruins

'Nick Dear's **The Art of Success** . . . may have been composed as a
romping and lubricious theatrical cartoon, with sexual desire wittily
put down whenever it raises a tentative head and anachronism
running rampant. But at its core the play grapples provocatively in
political and social terrain, while retaining high notes of comedy.'
Nicholas de Jongh, *Guardian*

Directed by Adrian Noble, **The Art of Success** was first performed by
the Royal Shakespeare Company at The Other Place, Stratford, in
1986 and subsequently transferred to The Pit, London, in 1987. It is
published here with **In the Ruins**, a two-hander, first broadcast on
BBC Radio 3 with Nigel Stock as George III. At the time of this volume
going to press, a production of this revised version was scheduled for
Bristol New Vic in Spring 1989.

Nick Dear was born in Portsmouth. For **The Art of Success** he won
the John Whiting Award and was nominated for a Laurence Olivier
Award. He was Playwright in Residence at the Royal Exchange,
Manchester, in 1987-8. His plays include **Food of Love** (Almeida
1988); **A Family Affair** (after Ostrovsky: Cheek by Jowl 1988); **The Art
of Success** (RSC 1986): **The Bed** (New York 1986); **Pure Science**
(RSC 1986); **Temptation** (RSC 1984); and **The Perfect Alibi**
(Colchester 1980). For BBC Radio he has written **Free** (1986);
Jonathan Wild (after Fielding, 1985); and **Matter Permitted** (1980),
for which he received a Pye Radio Award. Films include **The Ranter**
(1988); **The Monkey Parade** (1983); and **Memo** (1980).

Methuen New Theatrescripts series offers frontline intelligence of the most original and exciting work from the fringe.

authors in the same series

The Art of Success

In the Ruins

Two Plays by

Nick Dear

For Joan and for Peter

methuen

A Methuen New Theatrescript

This collection first published in Great Britain as a paperback original in 1989 by Methuen Drama, Michelin House, 81 Fulham Road, London SW3 6RB and distributed in the United States of America by HEB Inc, 70 Court St., Portsmouth, New Hampshire 03801.

The Art of Success *Copyright © Nick Dear 1989*
In the Ruins *Copyright © Nick Dear 1989*
This collection Copyright © Nick Dear 1989

British Library Cataloguing in Publication Data

Dear, Nick
    The art of success; and, In the ruins.
    I. Title
    822'.914

ISBN 0-413-61420-4

Printed in Great Britain by Expression Printers Ltd, London N7 9DP

The front cover illustration is a detail from Times of Day – Morning *by William Hogarth and is reproduced by kind permission of the Mary Evans Picture Library.*

Introduction

These two plays were conceived in the early nineteen-eighties, when I was living in rural West Yorkshire, the 'cradle of the industrial revolution'. Around me in the damp valleys lay the ruined architecture of the first machine age, now desolate and over-run with weed. And as northern Europe edged towards a post-industrial period, aided by a system of political thought which has seemed content not merely to bite the hand that raised it, but to torture it first, pull its fingernails off and dislocate its knuckles, I began to speculate on this business of passing from one age to another. What was life like before The Manufacturers appeared? And how do people respond to swift transition? These plays are both to do with moving on somewhere, fast, and coping with it well or not so well. They're about ambition and the search for tranquillity. For me they're a kind of diary.

In the Ruins was written first. I was trying to research William Hogarth when I ran into George the Third. He was talking so fast I had to stop and listen. Like everybody else I had a rough idea the old boy was mad, but I was surprised to discover the modern research which suggests that he suffered a disease we now know as porphyria. Since in my mind the notion of monarchy has always been indissolubly linked with insanity, I wrote a play about it without hardly stopping to think.

The Art of Success finally emerged from a flat overlooking the Thames at Wapping, shortly before the wharf below the window was 'redeveloped' to such an extent that where once had been a view of the river was now a view of rich peoples' real estate. London in the eighties is pure Hogarth in so many ways. I'd hear him muttering next to me as we walked through the City to Covent Garden, cursing at how you'll never get served in a bar near the Bank if you're not in a dark grey suit . . .

On the subject of cursing, the style of this piece has alarmed certain art history purists and self-appointed launderers of the nation's cultural underwear. Tough. I hate the way that creativity is sanitized for the coffee table, and it is inconceivable to me that William Hogarth did not have a filthy tongue in his head. Also, I started on the play with the guess that he couldn't have drawn brothels in such intimate detail had he not been familiar with them, and, well, the rest follows on from that. I have taken liberties with history, too. In my opinion there's far too much of it, so in this play I condensed ten years (1727-37) into the events of a single night. This tactic served to discompose all those who urgently wanted to know what the artist ate for breakfast the morning after finishing *Gin Lane*, but since this fraternity consisted almost entirely of persons writing for newspapers, I have lost no sleep over the complaint – principally because, like them, I never let the facts get in the way of a good story.

The text of **The Art of Success** was much improved in rehearsal by the contributions of the horribly talented original company. To them, my love and thanks.

Nick Dear
November 1988, Wales

The Art of Success

The Art of Success was first performed by the Royal Shakespeare Company at the The Other Place, Stratford upon Avon, on 2 July 1986. The play transferred to the Pit Theatre at the Barbican on August 13 1987. The cast was as follows:

Jane Hogarth	Niamh Cusack
William Hogarth	Michael Kitchen
Harry Fielding	Philip Franks
Frank	David Killick
Oliver	Simon Russell Beale
Mrs Needham	Dilys Laye
Louisa	Dinah Stabb
Sarah Sprackling	Penny Downie
Robert Walpole	Joe Melia
Queen Caroline	Susan Porrett

Other parts were played by members of the company.

Director Adrian Noble
Designer Ultz
Music Paul Reade

Act One

Scene I

London in the 1730s. The Beefsteak Club. A group of drunken men asleep at a table in the middle of the afternoon. They have collapsed amongst the debris of a huge meal. They snore contentedly.

*A Woman (**Jane**) enters stealthily. She circles the men in quiet anger. She makes out the one she's looking for (**William**). She raises a large pair of scissors, then puts them between **William**'s legs. There is a loud 'snip' and **William** wakes in panic. **Jane** exits. He doesn't see her.*

William No! Jane! Don't!

He jumps away from the table and examines himself, but nothing has happened to him.

Christ, what a bitch.

Harry *(waking)* What is it, Will?

William My wife, she –

William *looks under the table for her. She's not there.*

Nothing. A dream. My head is full of nightmares.

Harry It's the rich food and drink.

William It's the cuts of beef, the blood-red beef –

Harry The cheddar –

William The quantity of ale. The dreams get worse the more you gorge. It's as if the brain, it fractures open, and horrible creatures spew hot from its crack.

Harry I thought you said it was your wife.

William Well, yes, it was Janey, but she was – she had her dressmaking shears and she – well let's just say it's not what I had hoped for from a marriage.

Harry You regret it already?

William Don't talk daft.

Frank *(stirs and mumbles)* Minutes of the Annual General Meeting of . . .

Harry Tell me your dreams, if they're upsetting you.

William They're not upsetting me, nothing's upsetting me, there's just some bastard forever chipping away in my bloody sleep, carving away at my sense of myself, and why? Why? is it envy of my talent or what is it?

Harry It's all this boozing at lunchtime.

William I know, I know, and the pressure of work.

Harry And you have a lively imagination and you –

William Lively? It's running fucking riot, mate!

Frank (*stands, uncertainly, pissed*) Minutes of the Annual General Meeting of the Sublime Society of Beefsteaks, held in Mrs Needham's upstairs room this afternoon the –

Harry Meeting's adjourned, Frank.

Frank Normal agenda. Election of officers.

William Shut up, Frank.

Frank Officers re-elected without contest, as per last year. Minutes read and agreed with no dissent. Treasurer's report revealed a surplus in the bank and as per usual all new applications for membership of our estimable Club were unanimously rejected. Whereupon the Secretary volunteered the observation that the Society of Beefsteaks could well be said to mirror in little the happy torpor of our kingdom as a whole.

Harry Tell that to the poor of Dorset.

William Shut up, Harry.

Frank The membership thereupon with due and proper ceremony devoured the half-cooked rump of a bullock, sang several rather long songs of dubious tastefulness, burped a bit, farted a bit, and drank themselves into oblivion. (*Sits.*)

William A vote of thanks, to the Secretary.

Oliver (*his head on the table*) Seconded.

Frank (*rises*) Gratefully accepted. (*Sits.*)

William What about a small drink?

Frank (*rises*) We now proceed to Any Other Business, William.

Harry What's that, Frank?

William Oh no. Not me.

Oliver Hark at the newlywed.

William I don't want to catch nothing, do I.

Frank Wear your armour.

William I've chucked it away.

Frank They'll wash one out for you, I'm sure, they always have some spares.

Harry Spare what? What are you talking about?

Oliver The dried gut of a sheep.

Frank Cundums, boy. Are you telling us you've never worn one?

Harry No . . .

Frank Are you telling us you've never – had it off?

Harry No! But I've never been with a rented woman. Always gone with nice girls. When mother's back is turned. You don't fiddle about with a length of intestine in front of a girl from a genteel house. You discharge your obligations at once.

William Very gratifying.

Frank Dangerous, though.

William Not with your wife.

Frank Not with yours, perhaps. But my beloved . . . the sight of her unlaced would turn your thing to mush. (*Imploring.*) William . . .!

William No, I've got work to do before the daylight goes. And I said I'd meet Jane for a walk.

Frank A walk! The change in the man! Where once the fires of lust roared in his gut, now all is calm and sensible, a candle-flame of passion.

Harry I burn, though, Frank. I smoulder.

Frank You?

Harry Yes, I'm in the market. I believe a writer should sample every experience.

Frank Then I move: that this Annual General Meeting invite our good friend Mrs Needham to offer us a selection of her stock, the

Meeting having a view to purchase, and the necessary funds being made available by the Society.

Oliver   Seconded.

William   It's not coming out of the kitty?

Harry   Don't see why not. Treasurer's just seconded it.

William   (*outraged*) Fuck off!

Frank   William, this is a formally-constituted AGM, please speak through the chair if you have a point of order.

William   Are you trying to tell me that you lot intend getting your collective leg over and paying for it out of my bleeding subs?

Oliver   Yes, we are. Absolutely, yes.

William   Are you fuck! That's never fair!

Oliver   Yes it is.

William   What, you mean I lose out just because I love my wife?

Harry   Will –

William   What, mate?

Harry   You always *drink* more than your share. (*Laughter.*)

William   (*beaten*) You tight-fisted shits . . .

Oliver   Oh, stop complaining. Potter off home to the warmth of the bridal couch.

William   He desired my wife himself, you know. He would come sniffing round her doorway like an over-eager pup. When I was already inside.

Oliver   This kennel-talk is witty.

William   Is it. Then why don't you sod off and play with your bone?

Oliver   I'm only concerned for a fellow-member's welfare.

William   He's jealous!

Oliver   What is it, don't she come on heat quite as frequent as one might prefer? Or is it – dear Janey's a lovely tall bint, isn't she? – is it just too high for the mongrel to reach? I mean I've heard of marrying above oneself but this is –

Frank   Oliver –

Oliver – fucking ridiculous.

William (*makes a run at* **Oliver**) Come here, I'll cripple you!

William *is restrained by* **Frank** *and* **Harry**.

Oliver Oh, the upstart's frightfully drunk.

William Of course I'm drunk, what do you think I come here for, the company?

Oliver I am a peer of the realm – I could ruin your career!

William I'll pull your purple bollocks off, that'll fuck your pedigree!

Frank Gentlemen, please, behave like Beefsteaks! – Will, apologise to the Viscount.

Harry And Oliver, shake hands with a great artist.

Oliver A great artist? The runt with the inky fingers? A great artist? We talk a different language, Mr Fielding. Willy Hogarth, a great artist? Let us assess his curriculum vitae. What cathedrals has he done? What frescos of what battles? What mansion walls adorned with Roman heroes? What royal features stippled with immortal pigment?

William My portraits are widely reputed to be –

Oliver Oh, portraits, portraits, any hack can do titchy portraits to clutter up sideboards, but a great artist – Let me remind you one has toured the Continent and one has *seen* great art, I mean the originals, vast canvasses in gold leaf frames, huge blocks of stone chipped up to holiness, Annunciation, Pietà, and in the damp palaces of Venice spent my inheritance, spent money like water building my collection of Madonnas –

William Dead Christs, Holy Families, flying fucking angels, and ship-loads no doubt of similar dismal, dark subjects.

Oliver Historical allegories, mainly, drawn from the well of antique myth.

William Which no one can understand.

Oliver Not open to the common herd, I grant you.

William Which *I* can't understand.

Oliver Lack of education is such a dreary thing.

William   I didn't have time for an education, I had to earn a crust. I have no patron, no office, no inheritance, but what I do have is this body of work behind me, built from nothing. It's not great, not quite, but not inconsiderable, though I've flogged some shit I know, some rotten illustrations, but I do believe, I must allow myself to believe I have it in me – great work! Lasting work! I mean I am still learning, yes, I'm not exactly a prodigy, Christ, I hate prodigies, I've hated prodigies since I was about twenty-five years old, but fucking hell I'm making a fucking go of it, aren't I?

He goes and sits in a corner and sulks.

Oliver   . . . Something I said?

Harry   You ought to see his latest work, it's bloody good.

Oliver   Oh? What is the subject?

Harry   A harlot.

Oliver   A harlot? What, a tart? Oh, jolly well done, Will, a picture of a tart –

William   Six pictures.

Oliver   Six?

Harry   He calls it a Progress.

Oliver   Six pictures of a whore? Progress? That is utterly silly. What chap of any character or standing is going to want to be seen buying six pictures of a prostitute, for heaven's sake?

Harry   Well, I've ordered a set of prints.

Frank   Me too, the wife wants some.

Oliver   Oh, prints, well, prints, absolutely, naturally one shall have a set of prints oneself, but one is talking about paintings, canvasses, one is talking about art. Art rests in the original, not the copy.

Harry   Does it?

Oliver   Why certainly. Anyone can own a copy. Genius is not shared around like a bag of peppermints.

Frank   Buy the originals, then. You've got the cash.

William   They're not for sale. Not to him, who covets my wife.

Oliver   See? He's petrified.

William (*returning*) Of what am I petrified?

Oliver That your work will not stand compare with the fruits of my Grand Tour. How can a man who has barely been south of the Thames seriously aspire to be a painter?

William What is art?

Oliver Now let's not split hairs.

William No, what is art – property? Or communication? Does it exist to be owned, or to be understood?

Oliver I think I'll just nip downstairs and have a word with Mrs Needham.

William Do you know what I'm talking about?

Oliver No, damn you, but I know what I like.

William And what do you like?

Oliver Well . . . As a rule, William . . . Something with a certain 'je ne sais quoi', that's what I usually go for.

Exit **Oliver** *with a superior air.*

Frank That is the great benefit of a Club such as ours. The interchange of ideas between men of civilisation and intelligence. – A picture's a picture, I would have said.

William But what if every bloke in the street can own a masterpiece for sixpence? Then where are your connoisseurs? Your gentlemen collectors?

Frank I never imagined you as a champion of the heaving masses.

William Champion my arse. I want their sixpences. I reckon I can as well get a living by dealing with the public in general, as by hanging on the whims and fancies of the rich. In fact I could be very wealthy.

Frank Then why aren't you?

William Because of the pirates. The bastard pirates of print. Some geezer will come round my place posing as a buyer for the original painting, and the next thing you know there'll be a shoddy bloody copy of it in the shops before I've even got the acid off my etching, and then they'll knock down my payments because the market's flooded with imitations it makes you weep!

Frank But surely you have copyright on your design?

Harry No, he doesn't, because it's very hard to legislate for the ownership of an idea. The thunder and lightning in your head. Writers were only granted protection of our ideas a few years ago. There's nothing that covers the specific problems of engravers.

Frank I'm only a simple merchant. The world of art is strange to me, all I know anything about is life. Now, in life, if I've a boat-load of sugar, say, or blacks, or molasses, I expect to have a document to prove I own the cargo, and I don't expect a soul to challenge it, or if they do that's stealing and they'll hang. We have greatly widened the scope of the capital offence under Mr Walpole. Can you identify your pirates?

William Course I can, they're all old mates.

Frank Then you must have redress.

William What, you mean like, take them round the back of the printshop and –

Frank No, man, in the courts! Go through the courts! Use the law, it's made for you. Whether you like it or not you're a businessman now.

William (*thoughtful*) Art as business. Yes.

Harry But you'd have to get the law *changed,* Frank. You'd have to get a Bill through parliament.

Frank Then petition parliament. That's what it's for. It's made up of perfectly ordinary fellows, Harry, very like me if the truth be known, and very understanding of another fellow's needs.

Harry You mean it's a corrupt little clique whose sole reason for existence is to line its own pockets.

William Run by Robert Walpole . . .

Harry Precisely, that's why I ridicule him in every play I've ever written. In the new one I represent him as a – (midget)

Frank Don't tell me, don't spoil it, I'm coming to the show! Oliver and I are going to drum up some trade for you.

Harry What, tonight? Thanks very much.

Frank (*to* **William**) No doubt you've satirised the Great Man as well, have you? It being so much the fashion.

William No, not him personally, I haven't.

Harry Then now's your chance, Will! What a chance! 'The Harlot's Progress' is going to be a huge success. Why don't you follow it up with a political one? Why don't you do a 'Statesman's Progress' and drag our tyrant through the mud?

William No.

Harry Why not? Depicting how he bribed his way to power?

William No.

Harry It'll sell in tens of thousands!

William There are more important things in life than money, Henry!

Harry Yes, I'm talking about them!

William I said no, didn't I?

Harry But you never said why not.

William Look, I know you're my best mate and all –

Harry Well, I used to be.

William But if there's one thing I won't do it's peddle second-hand ideas, Harry, because I'm not interested in theories, I'm interested in people – you get bogged down in theory you never reach into yourself –

Harry We're above it, are we? We're untouched by the world?

William Nobody tells me what to paint! – I'm bursting for a slash. (*Exit.*)

Frank Ah, the tactical widdle, veteran of many a boardroom skirmish.

Harry (*bitter*) Interested in people . . . ! I remember a time when no one was safe from the blade of his graving-tool. The rich and the mighty and the idiotic chiselled out in black and white. Simple monochrome of judgement.

Frank Attack, attack, attack, it's all attack with you. Some things are worth defending – stable government for one. Learn a little balance, or the Prime Minister will close you down.

Harry He can't, I'm far too popular.

William (*returning*) The bucket's gone – what shall I do?

Frank Into the street. I think I'll join you.

Harry Now you come to mention it –

All three piss out of the window with sighs of relief.

Frank Bet you a tanner you can't get it in that window.

Pause.

William You owe me a tanner.

They giggle. Unseen by them, **Mrs Needham** *enters with* **Oliver***. She peers at the men.*

Needham You'll get another drop out of that if you wring it.

Frank Mrs Needham!

The pissers are embarrassed.

Needham We, too, live in the sight of God, remember. This is a respectable street! How would you like it if I came and urinated over your neighbours? (*They all approve of the idea.*) Cheeky devils. What is it you want, then? Don't be bashful, we must have a proper order. The goods are stored below, it only remains to make a requisition. (*She takes out a notebook and checks off a list.*) May God forgive me what I do. My constant prayer is that I might make enough from this commerce to leave off in good time to atone. You, young man, what sort of a slut is your heart's desire? (**Harry** *gawps.*) They're all quite clean and they go to church on Sundays. I've got Peggy free, she's a little fat one, she will rub you in her bosom till you come off in her face, she doesn't mind, she's used to it, what do you say to that?

Harry Er, I –

Needham Good, that's you sorted.

Frank Elizabeth – don't make it difficult for us.

Needham It's not me making it difficult, Frank, it's the Lord. And I hope you've lost your taste for stinging nettles. I had a rash for a week.

Frank You weren't holding them right. If you hold them right you don't get stung.

Needham That's if you hold them with your hands, Frank. Now then, you sir – what can I tempt you with? Birch twigs? Leather face-mask? Would you care to join a filthy masquerade?

William No, I don't think I would, thank you.

Needham Boys, is it? I've got boys if you want them.

William No it isn't boys! It's – I – it's because I – oh, fuck.

The others laugh at him. Stumped for an explanation, he turns and leaves angrily.

Needham Some people shock very easy. But not my favourite Viscount. I have a treat for a regular customer. I have a little virgin, a real one mind, nothing sewn up or otherwise embroidered, an innocent young beauty I've been schooling in the sciences of lust, and for an extra guinea you may shag her infant brains out, if you wish . . .

Pause. **Oliver** *takes out his purse and drops it on the table. Blackout.*

Scene II

A pleasure garden. Amongst the classical statuary and symmetrical borders stands **Louisa**, *on the lookout for trade.*

Louisa (*shivers*) Wind off the Thames blows down the avenues, round the rotunda, through the triumphal arches and directly up my skirt. I must have the coldest legs in England. A sailor in a Bermondsey cellar said that in China they tell of a wind disease, a cold, cold wind blowing round the body, typhoon in your arms and legs, whispering draughts at the back of your skull. I told him I think I've got it, mate, it all sounds dead familiar. He laughed and bit my nipple with splintering teeth. What I would have loved, at that moment, what I longed for, was that all the air would whoosh out of me like a burst balloon, and I sink down to nothing at his feet, and teach the disbelieving rat a lesson. Here I am out in all weathers, all the entrances and exits in my body open to the elements day and freezing night, what's to stop the gale when it comes in and fills me? And blows round my bones for ever? – Wait, is he walking this way? That dragoon? He looks so sad . . . doesn't he look sad . . . I don't know, they call this place a pleasure garden, I've never seen such misery, I'd christen it the garden of wind and disappointment, or cold and frosted cunt.

Jane *has entered, unseen. She listens.*

Is he coming over here? Come along, then, miss, get all your gusts and breezes together . . . Nice time with an old windbag, soldier? It's not wearing any knickers.

She promenades. She sees **Jane**.

And what do you want, may I ask?

Jane Aren't you cold? You look blue.

Louisa Well who's going to want to shaft a shiverer wrapped from head to foot in rags. You have to show a man a bit of skin.

Jane Why don't you wear some stockings, at least?

Louisa (*mimes being strangled*) That's why. And they never see the goose-pimples. Lust is a great blinder, oh isn't it just. – Oh farts, he's wandering off. That was you done that. He must've thought we're only working doubles.

Jane I do beg your pardon. I couldn't help overhearing – I couldn't tear myself away. Please let me give you some money.

Louisa What have I got to do for it?

Jane Why, nothing. Take it. You have the most appalling life, don't you?

Louisa . . . Are you looking for an unusual experience?

Jane Um, I don't think so.

Louisa Because it makes me livid. Young ladies of quality coming down here, all for an hour of rough sex.

Jane Oh dear.

Louisa Taking the bread right out of our mouths!

Jane You have my sympathy.

Louisa Good. (*She hits* **Jane**.) Then perhaps you'll heed a gentle warning. Stay off my patch! You won't enjoy it. Soft skin bruise up like a peach. And what about the bite-marks and the blood?

Jane You misunderstand, I'm waiting for my – (husband.)

Louisa *hits her again.*

Ow! – I suppose if you are forced to live like an animal you are going to start to behave like one.

Louisa Don't call me an animal. Animals don't do this for a living.

William *enters.*

William Janey, there you are.

Jane You're late. I've had to send the carriage away and I've had to wait here alone.

Louisa (*staring pointedly at* **William**) I don't know you from somewhere, do I, sir?

William (*rigid with panic*) I shouldn't think so, no.

Jane My husband is actually rather famous. It is possible you may have had him pointed out to you in town.

Louisa That must be it. I thought he looked familiar.

Jane He is an artist.

Louisa Well isn't that a nice thing to be. A profession as old as my own.

Jane William this poor woman is a prostitute.

William Oh, is she?

Jane She is forced to solicit for custom even in this foul weather. Isn't that shaming? To you, I mean? A man? – What is your name?

Louisa Louisa, madam.

Jane Louisa I hold nothing against you. But for the accident of birth I . . . Oh, the trade in flesh, isn't it pernicious.

William Yes but there's nothing we can do about it today.

Jane Perhaps there is. Perhaps if we took this woman home and gave her a hot meal and a bath, she might regain her – (self respect.)

William You're joking!

Louisa (*shivers tragically*) The wind . . . The wind blows through the warmest men, and turns their hearts as cold as stone. There's a bloke over there by the Temple of Virtue, I think he's wanting business. Excuse me. (*Exit, flashing a leg at* **William**.)

Jane And where I wonder will she sleep tonight?

William Up Drury Lane by the Queen's Head, that's – oh – that's where they all live, Janey, isn't it? Up Drury Lane? Them back alleys?

Jane I brought your basket. With roast beef and beer. – Will, you don't have anything to do with such women, do you? Not now we're together?

William No, never, never, I swear it. Temptation comes my way sometimes but I am strong and I resist it. Save myself for you. And your little cheeks red from the wind. (*Kisses her.*)

Jane Imagine them out here . . . brr! . . . having to . . .

William (*interested*) What?

Jane You know. Up against the trees, the rough bark in your hair, linen down in the leaf-mould . . .

William You find it – exciting?

Jane Not so much exciting as just –

William Dirty.

Jane A tightness at the back of the throat and I –

William Sordid.

Jane Well . . .

William But somewhere down in the dregs of your mind you –

Jane Yes – ?

William Jane I love you, let's get on the floor.

Jane I beg your pardon!

William It's not very wet.

He tries to drag her down.

Jane William! Are you out of your mind!

William Yes, yes, I'm berserk for you, come on darling, you're my prize –

Jane This is a public place!

William – my reward for being good, give it to me Janey –

Jane I'm sorry but I can't!

William – open your lovely knees!

Jane *breaks away. Pause.*

Jane I thought we were going out for a walk . . . !

William Oh, fuck.

Jane What sort of woman . . . What sort of woman is it you want me to be? You seem to want to make me something I am not.

William I'm trying. I am trying! There aren't many men who understand women at all, you know.

Jane Understand women . . . ?

William Yes, well, I'm making a bleeding effort, at least.

Jane An effort?

William Yes an effort! Do I force you? Do I ever? Hot with humiliation in the Vauxhall mud and do I complain? No, I try to understand.

Jane He thinks he understands. Hallelujah! Pass the paintpot! Pass the pedestal, let me get on! – God, the limitless arrogance of them.

William Thanks very much, Jane, that's just the gesture of support I was hoping for.

Jane I love you, I love you, idiot! But you take so much for granted! That I will need you when you need me. That I will be clean but dirty, ignorant but clever. That I will have a mind of my own that you can say you're proud of. Loving you is such a struggle . . . hand-to-hand every inch of the way . . . I am enmeshed in you, and I don't always like it. But it happens! It happens! I am a tangle of things not easily unravelled. So please, don't go round thinking you begin to understand me. Just love me. That's all. Just accept. Because I refuse to be understood.

William (*pause. He averts his eyes*) I'll see you tonight.

Exit **William** *with basket.* **Jane** *takes a step after him, then stops with a gesture of anger and frustration. Fade to black.*

Scene III

A prison cell. Piles of dirt and straw. A high barred window and heavy door. A table and chair, and a stool. **Sarah** *sits at the table, sunk in daydreams. There is a woman's cry, far away in the depths of the gaol.* **Sarah** *comes to, blinking. She pays no attention to the cry. She empties the contents of a jug of water into a bowl: about half a cupful. With a sigh of annoyance she rolls up her sleeves and prepares to wash herself. Then changes her mind, picks* *up the bowl and goes to drink. Then changes her mind again, puts it down, and washes her grimy arms and face. When finished she looks into the water with distaste. She arranges her filthy clothes as neatly as she can. She has a silver spoon concealed in a pocket. She polishes it up and checks her reflection. She smells her breath, pokes at a rotting tooth. She puts the spoon away and looks at the water again. Then in one swift movement she grabs the bowl, drinks the water, and sets it back on the table again as if it hadn't happened. She stares ahead with an innocent look. The bolts on the far side of the door are drawn back. A* **Gaoler** *shows* **William** *into the cell. He carries his basket. He sniffs the air and recoils.*

Sarah You came then. I weren't sure.

She extends her hand to him.

Gaoler Sir, the fever in a gaol . . . They say you feel it dance beneath the skin . . . Like a fire in a turf-moor, never put it out. If you're lucky you go mad before you die.

William Cheers, I look forward to it. (*Shakes* **Sarah**'s *hand.*)

Gaoler I have to bolt the door, has this been explained?

William Yes, but do it quietly, I've got a miserable headache and I'm not in a very good mood.

Gaoler You can still change your mind.

William I've been in a nick before. Grew up in the shadow of the walls. Father a debtor, poor old bugger. Done well for myself, though, haven't I? (*Shows off his clothes.*)

Gaoler Yes, sir, you have.

William Obviously being terrorised at an impressionable age by shits with whips and manacles provides a first-rate training for the wider world.

Sarah *laughs. The* **Gaoler** *turns nasty.*

Gaoler I'm going to lock you in, now, sir, in the bowels of Newgate, all right?

The **Gaoler** *leaves and locks the door.*

Sarah It is an honour to meet you.

William The light in here is rubbish. Rubbish.

Sarah Your eyes soon get accustomed.

William But the smell – the excrement of fear – that takes me back.

Sarah I'm sorry about the pong but –

William Don't be.

Sarah – there's an open sewer –

William Dung does not disgust me. Quite the contrary. It reminds us what we are. I refuse to let myself be offended by any human functions.

Sarah Very nice it must be, having the choice.

William I see you have a flicker of wit. How would you like to be – preserved?

Sarah Don't care.

William Course you do.

Sarah No I don't.

William Are you going to mess me about?

Sarah I don't care!

William But your appearance – you've gone to some trouble – I'm amazed you can keep as clean as that in this fuck-awful place. The power of a woman's self-respect! – Or am I being condescending, sorry if I am.

Sarah I ain't gone to any bother.

William Sit you at the table I think. (*She sits.*) Background of barred window and bolted door. I'd like to do something with the stench. The way the air hangs heavy with disease, drip of plague like dew . . . But how do you show a smell, I wonder? How do you paint an aroma?

Sarah You can't, it's impossible.

William Not if you have any art. You might for example draw someone holding a scented handkerchief to their nose, standing nearby and, what could they be – glancing at the pisspot?

Sarah How do we know it is scented?

William What?

Sarah This hankie. This feller, he could be just blowing.

William Perfume bottle –

Sarah Oh, good.

William – peeping from the pocket of his coat.

William *sits on the stool and prepares his sketching board.*

Sarah You got a bit of a brain, too, haven't you?

William Ta, yes, as a nipper I was apprenticed to a silver engraver, my widowed mum being very poor, and since then I've developed this system of like visual language, this technical memory, which is unique in that it –

Sarah How do I know it is perfume?

William What?

Sarah In the bottle.

William Well of course it's perfume.

Sarah Could be water.

William Well it's not.

Sarah Could be gin.

William It's perfume!

Sarah But how do I know?

William Because it's written on the side! 'Perfume'!

Sarah No it's not.

William It is, it is!

Sarah (*bangs table*) Look, prick, it's bloody well not.

William (*wary of her*) . . . Why not?

Sarah Cause I can't bloody well read, that's why not. Is it so much, that I should understand?

Pause. **William** *begins to work.*

William Sketching in chalk and pencil, Sarah. Won't take long. Sorry I was late, been rushing round town all day, I'm so bloody busy it's not real. On my way here I thought I would put in the Gaoler. With his keys and whip. But that would kind of prejudge the case, wouldn't it?

Sarah Good, I can live without him breathing down me neck.

William Does he pester you? I could have a word with the Governor or someone.

Sarah He daren't come near me. He's scared I cut his throat. (*Laughs.*) Would too. That brute. I seen him rub his self. He'll prob'ly wait till I'm done for, then he'll stick it in. Then he'll turn me over to the surgeons.

William Haven't you got no family to –

Sarah What, hang on me legs? They say it's a blessing if you can get someone to hang on your legs, don't they? Speeds things up considerable.

William I meant – to take the body. And bury you.

Sarah Not in this parish. Or if I have I've forgotten 'em. (*Pause.*) Another life. Like a dream now. (*Pause.*) They'll have me on the butcher's slab and set to with the chopper. I'll be splayed out there like a lump of meat, I'll have no defence, clamp me knees together they'll chop 'em off, slice my thighs to rashers, and there's my honour up for grabs. And off with her hands. And off with her noisy old head. And now I am dismembered by a dozen men, me giblets all over the floor, and they have their leathery fingers in me in the name of science, searching for the bit that went bad.

William (*aghast*) How can you talk like that?

Sarah How? Damn, if I got to think it, every other bugger will too.

William . . . I don't half pity you.

Sarah You after the bad bit, too? That what you come here to paint? The evil, the rot, and that?

William Well, I'm just doing a sketch.

Sarah I can throw a fit if you like.

William (*interested*) Oh? What sort of a fit?

Sarah I don't know, a mad fit. (*She rolls her eyes.*)

William And what's the effect of that?

Sarah Scares the shite out of magistrates, mainly. (*Laughs. Subsides.*) Something bubbles up inside me, I don't know.

William (*disapproving*) But we all have these urges, and we all have to contain them.

Sarah Why?

William Don't ask stupid questions, it's bleeding obvious, isn't it?

Sarah Why?

William Well – for fear of what the law will do to us otherwise!

Sarah But I am a law to myself. Now. The judges have run out of punishments.

William Oh, Christ, how can you argue against it? – You have to have respect for the law, Sarah.

Sarah You're not getting fucking hung in the morning. – How is it out, is it wet?

William It's windy, with the last of an autumn sun.

Sarah I bet it rains tomorrow then. Now, I shall sit like a proper lady so's you feel at your ease. I want you to do your best work. You can imagine for yourself the lapdog and the velvet and the little negro feller with the studded silver collar and you can put them in when you get back home. Just get the essence of me for now. (*Pause.*) I'll sit as still as still. (*Pause.*) Like I sat after I done the killings. Ever so peaceful. Not thinking no more. Calm as a duck on a pond. God there is such relief in murder . . . ! (*Pause.*) The dogs stop baying in your head. – I ain't alarming you, am I, Mr Hogarth, you seem to have stopped . . .?

William Yes . . . you are . . . slightly.

Sarah Why, whatever sort of a person do you think I am?

William You're a murderess.

Sarah Oh, *that.* I have my better side. Jesus, I wasn't born killing.

Without warning, she gets up, hoists her skirts, and squats over a bucket.

William Oi!

Sarah What?

William What the fuck are you playing at? (*He looks closely.*)

Sarah Won't be a tic.

William That's indecent, a woman piddling in public.

Sarah I don't care.

William That's obscene.

Sarah All done now. (*She resumes her pose at the table.*)

William . . . Haven't you got no shame?

Sarah It's a blank, it's all a blank. Decency, dignity, pride. A sour piss in a rusty bucket. From the moment I picked up the razor. To the moment my feet swing through the air. A blank. Get drawing, then, it's getting dark.

William I hate despair, I really do.

Sarah I ain't despairing. It's just all one to me. This world, it don't change. I just don't fight against it no more. – Here, what you got in that basket?

William That's for later.

Sarah What's for later? Is it me food?

William Do you want your picture taken down or not?

Sarah I want to know why a famous high society painter wants to do a portrait of silly old me.

William Well, I'm recently married, I need the cash.

Sarah Why you bothering with me, then? I haven't got none.

William It's business, that's all. I'm a businessman.

Sarah And I thought you were an artist.

William I'm an artist who likes to eat.

Sarah What've you brung me? What?

William So you *can* be tempted . . . Something in you stirs . . .

Sarah It's me belly, it's going mad!

William Let's finish the sketch first, shall we? Then eat?

Sarah I'm destroyed with hunger, root and branch I wither, look at me droop, me neck'll be slipping out the noose at this rate and you'll be to blame, go on, give us a crust to chew on while you're working.

William No, you wouldn't keep still. (**Sarah** *groans.*) I haven't got for ever, have I? It's not as if I can come back next week and re-do your great chomping gob!

Sarah *stands.*

William   I'm sorry, I'm sorry –

Sarah *goes to a dark corner of the cell.*

Where exactly do you think you're off to?

Sarah   I can get out of the light, at least.

William   But you made your mark on a legal paper. Your consent.

Sarah   Don't mean a thing to me. I can't read.

William   Look, do you want your place in fucking history or don't you?

Sarah   I am about to die, I think I am entitled to a bite to eat!

William (*considers the situation*)   Miss . . . 'Sorry' is a remarkable word, isn't it? In the few months I've lived with my wife I've begun to see the value of it. Every little petty quarrel can be sorted. Jane tries to make me see the female point of view. I would have said to ask forgiveness was unmanly. My fists were permanently clenched. My jaw thrust in to any barney. But now I can be meek as a bleeding lamb when the need arises. Give me two more minutes. Please. You did make your cross!

Sarah (*suddenly returns*)   Well! Who is this woman who can work such wonders?

William   Her father is Sergeant-Painter to the King.

Sarah   Oh, married the boss's daughter.

William   Don't be so cheeky.

Sarah   I see now how you got in with the nobs.

William   I did not marry for reasons of commerce. I married for love. However I do have a new series of paintings on view at my house, inspired by some ideas of my wife's, which I've reason to believe may make me a fortune.

Sarah   Why've you come here then?

William   You are notorious. I think there may be a quick profit in it. I have a lot of debts.

Sarah (*smiles*)   . . . As long as people see that I am bad. I want to be bad. That's how I want to be remembered. As an insult. A spit in the face. Do me like that. (**William** *nods.*) I could kill you for the food, I s'pose . . . But I can't be bothered. Not after I just had a wash.

They both resume their seats.

William Christ what a day. (*He draws.*)

Sarah A blunt razor I used to kill the old women. The widow's memento of her long-dead man. I was that ravenous, I had ceased to think, and that felt good, you can think too much when you're starving. I knew that my mistress's treasure was under her cot. So I bled the bitch and her bedmate while they slept. (*Laughs.*) Two stuck pigs in their petticoats. The rage, the urge to eat crept over me, and I succumbed. The peacefulest moment I ever have known . . . that second I abandoned trying to be good. You throw off the wretched, useless rags you've gone cold in all your life – the common sense, the reason – throw it to the wind and go naked, raw, free suddenly . . . Then Mary, the maid, with who I shared the attic, appeared on the stair, so I had to kill her too, aren't you done yet?

William *is sitting with his chalk held in mid-air. Then he scrawls on the bottom of the paper, and is finished.*

William (*quiet*) The two old women, yes, I kind of understand, I read that they mistreated you . . . but the maid? Why the maid? Why on earth?

Sarah Shrieked at the blood, soppy cow. I knew that if I was committing the perfect crime I could scarce afford to leave a witness.

William . . . Why'd you get caught then?

Sarah Ah. Don't know. I can't explain things. Not in words. I never even managed to sell the damn silver. So hunger follows me down to the lime-pit.

William (*sickened*) Women killing women . . .

Sarah Don't men kill men? – Can I have a look, then?

Wearily, **William** *puts his sketch in front of her. He takes a bottle of beer from the basket and drinks.*

William Understand, it's not finished, it's only a rough –

Sarah Me?

William I'll work it up in the studio, oh sod I hate it the first time they –

Sarah That – is me?

William That is a – preliminary version of you.

Sarah *takes out her spoon, polishes it, stares at the picture, stares at her reflection, stares at the picture again.*

Sarah It's warped.

William No, the spoon's warped, the spoon distorts –

Sarah That's a good silver spoon! Are you telling me I look like that?

William I'm not completely useless with a stick of chalk.

Sarah Liar!

William What's this, criticism?

Sarah Look at her with the little pout and the sparkle in the corner of her eye. The face is hard but. But! Do I ever sit like that with my damn knees apart? I do not. You give me desire. I have none!

William It's the best I could manage.

Sarah But the whole blasted reason I'm in here in the first place is that I would not whore! And you gone and made me one! Oh, there's plenty of room in the brothels for hungry farmgirls, plenty of quick shillings to be earned in cold and dingy courtyards, but would I descend to it? – no I had my respect, dullwit I now see myself to be, I lived like a beast but I wouldn't sell *that*!

William My head is throbbing, will you pipe down? I must say in my defence it said in the newspapers that –

Sarah The newspapers are the main reason I have never bothered to learn to read.

William You are described as a laundress.

Sarah Possibly because I am one.

William But you can't make a living as a laundress, can you? Too many people are content to go dirty.

Sarah But I've a right to a reputation like anyone else!

William Look, I'm an artist, an artist must be free to view the world unhindered.

Sarah Why?

William Well he can't let his subjects dictate to him!

Sarah Why not?

William Christ you're impossible.

Sarah You have made me some creation of your own. Warped what you see sitting here. You *assumed*. You are a prick. And what's this squiggle at the bottom?

William (*picks up sketch*) That? Oh, that's my signature. So people know it's authentic. (*Explains.*) By me.

Sarah . . . What people?

William The ones who'll come to look when I exhibit the finished painting.

Sarah Where?

William In my house in Covent Garden.

Sarah Never. I want it destroyed.

William Oh, please don't be difficult.

Sarah You got me mad now.

William It's just one bloody thing after another. (*He gathers his things up.*)

Sarah It's not how I want to go down! In the future! I told you, I want to look evil, I feel evil, I got demons in me and where are they in this balls-up? I want to be bad! Through and through! Not fallen angel! Not mildewed rose! Now give it back!

William I am truly sorry, Sarah, but it's mine, I own it, I hold a thing called the copyright you see. I must be going now. I have a pressing appointment. Why don't you help yourself to supper?

He hammers on the door. It's quite dark in the cell now.

Sarah It is *my* picture. *My* picture. Picture of *me*.

William (*calls*) William Hogarth! Open up!

Sarah (*calm*) Give me my likeness back, you are stealing it, you are taking my soul.

William Sarah . . . Believe me . . . I am so sorry for you.

A horrible wailing noise, the screaming of women, very loud. **William** *clutches at his head.* **Sarah** *is still.*

Oh . . . ! What's that?

Suddenly, from the shadows in the corners of the cell, a number of nightmarish **Women Prisoners** *emerge and run at* **William**. *They clutch at him. He tries to get away, yelling for the* **Gaoler**. *All the time this dreadful noise, half-pain, half-laughter.* **Sarah** *remains still. The cell door clangs open. The* **Gaoler** *stands brandishing his whip. The prisoners, except* **Sarah**, *disappear.* **William** *runs out with the picture.* **Sarah** *falls on the basket and stuffs food into her mouth. She bends over, retching. The* **Gaoler** *goes up to her.*

Gaoler   Here, love, you all right? What's the matter, can't your stomach take it?

Sarah *comes up in a swift movement and gets her arm round the* **Gaoler***'s neck. Her other hand comes up from the basket with a small knife in it. She slits his throat. He falls and dies.*

Sarah   Mad I said. Good and mad.

She picks up the **Gaoler***'s bunch of keys. Blackout.*

Scene IV

Louisa*'s lodging.* **William** *is asleep, sprawled in a chair, a glass of red wine clutched in his lap and tilting dangerously.* **Louisa** *enters, taking off her shawl. She sees him. She groans inwardly. She goes to him and removes his wig from his head. He mutters in his sleep.*

William   The faces . . . Those faces . . .

Louisa *smoothes his cropped hair. She tries to take the glass out of his hand but he won't let go. She kneels in front of him and starts to prise his fingers open. He hangs on so tightly that he wakes up. Seeing* **Louisa** *kneeling between his legs, he fears the worst. He leaps away in panic.*

What, again? Why can't you leave me alone?

Louisa   You were spilling your drink.

William   Lou . . . ? Louisa? Is it you? Am I awake?

Louisa   You were dreaming. Your eyes flicking back and forth beneath the lids. Like a lizard on a pebble.

William   Had to come. Couldn't keep away no longer.

Louisa (*sighs*) I've only just knocked off work.

William I've had a pig of a day and all. I've been locked up in Newgate Gaol. I'm doing a print of Sarah Sprackling. (*He has it rolled up in his pocket.*) Plan to have an edition on sale straight after the poor woman's turned off. Get in while she's still fresh in the public imagination – all those crowds who will bay at the hanging – last portrait of the deceased – got to be an earner. So I went down to her dungeon to sketch a design for the engraving and I – I can't describe them, there were these females – they come at me and – their faces! The eyes of them!

Louisa Sit down, Will.

William Feels like the seams are splitting in my head, the skin tight on the skull . . . !

Louisa Let Louisa make it better. (*She cradles his head.*)

William The dreams are bad enough, but waking visions – Christ!

Louisa You can always come to me, you know that.

William I know I can, Lou, I haven't been since the wedding because I –

Louisa Don't have to explain. I understand.

William You do, I know you do.

Pause.

Louisa What's her father like? The Sergeant-Painter?

William Oh, you know who she is, then?

Louisa Well, today was the first time we'd been formally introduced, but I like to keep myself in the picture, yes.

William He's not a bad bloke. We have a natter up the scaffold in St Paul's – he's doing the inside of the dome. We get along all right, but I don't feel I'm in the presence of a fellow-genius, if you know what I mean.

Louisa I know what you mean.

William Not everyone does.

Louisa You're not very happy, dear, are you?

William No I'm not. I know I ought to be. That makes it worse.

Louisa Do you talk to anyone else about it?

William Who for example?

Louisa I don't know. Your friends?

William I haven't got any. I have allies, yes. I don't have friends.

Louisa Well, what about the wife? Can't you confide in her? I thought that's what they were for, baring of the soul and what have you. – No?

William Well, she's young, isn't she, she's a lot younger than you or me, mate, there are things I wouldn't want to burden her with, seeing she's –

Louisa You mean she doesn't know about –

William – a respectable girl from a good background who –

Louisa – how you like your lover to –

William – is deeply in love with me and –

Louisa – piss and shit in your –

William Well of course not, she's my wife! I stood up with her in a bleeding church, I can't ask her to do that! She's a decent, well-bred girl!

Louisa Then presumably she doesn't push her finger in your bottom when you –

William No she doesn't, of course she doesn't, she wouldn't know where to start!

Louisa So we're not completely satisfied with married life . . . ?

William Not completely, no!

Louisa Husbands . . . Out there in the world you seem so capable, on top of things, the man in the saddle. But in my dingy bedrooom . . . the dark, wild longings . . . stampede of forbidden desires . . . secret needs which you'll only admit –

William Oh, the sex in my dreams!

Louisa – to your whore.

William My erections in the dead of night, dear Christ, like wood, like stone!

Louisa Sometimes I think I understand men. What a mistake that is. A woman will talk to another woman about what gives her pleasure. In this trade, we have to work at if it we want anything for ourselves, so we swap ideas, trying to . . . remember . . . – But the way you lot carry on you'd think it was against the law to admit you'd got your dick up. Probably is, come to think of it.

William Listen, I had this dream –

Louisa You are paying the going rate, are you, Will?

William What, after all these years?

Louisa Yes.

William Jesus. – A little old woman was sucking me off –

Louisa Is this a dream or a nursery rhyme?

William A little old lady, yes, I thought it repulsive at first but then I got to quite enjoy it. But then it turned – my whatsit – turned into this kind of brittle, burnt-up sausage effort, and it broke off in her mouth, all flaky and crumbly, and she munched away at it until it was gone. Completely gone! I looked down to see if another one was growing. At first I had only a bit of a stump. Fuck, I thought, that's the last time I'm unfaithful. But then I saw I had a little winkle like a little boy's. It was growing back. I was turning into some kind of reptile.

Louisa (*laughs*) Perhaps that means you've got a hidden fear of –

William Don't try and interpret it! I'm not interested in interpreting it! I'm interested in making it go away! – Another time I was making love with a man. And I enjoyed it. In the dream. How am I supposed to explain all this to Jane? She thinks I'm a great painter. She thinks I'm an idealist!

Louisa Someone ought to put her straight.

William Well that's not very friendly.

Louisa And why should I be? Once, way back in the mists of time, you spoke love, whispered love . . .

William (*quiet*) Heat of the moment, darling.

Louisa Thought I was getting out of it . . . New life dawning and all that bunk.

A drum roll, off.

Drummer (*off*) Announcing, tonight at the Haymarket, at prices to suit every pocket –

William   Oh God. Harry's play.

Drummer (*off*)   A brand new farce by Mr Henry Fielding!

A parade enters and marches round the auditorium. It comprises a **Woman Drummer**, *wearing a fancy bonnet and a flowing skirt, and beating a large drum which sways on her hip;* **Harry Fielding**, *separated from the main group;* **Oliver; Frank; Mrs Needham;** *and a* **Man** *in a comic mask from a masquerade.* **Louisa** *and* **William** *look out at the procession, but the* **Marchers** *do not acknowledge them.*

Harry   A dozen years? Fifteen? How long has the bastard been in power? How long will you stand for it?

William   Christ, he's pissed as a rat.

Harry   Butterfly-like he flits from crown to crown, with his tongue in the nation's honey!

Louisa   He'll get himself arrested.

William   It's pathetic. Why can't he face up to reality? Oh, you can make a big noise, let all the world know how radical you are, but then down comes the polished boot of power – prevents you from doing your work!

Louisa   You don't have to justify yourself to me.

Harry   Listen to this catalogue of corruption: 'First Lord of the Treasury, Mr Walpole. First Lord of the Admiralty, Mr Walpole. Clerk of the Pells, Mr Walpole's son. Customs of London, second son of Mr Walpole.'

William   But in my silence I am eloquent you see. I keep on turning it out.

Harry   'Secretary to the Treasury, Mr Walpole's brother. Postmaster General, Mr Walpole's other brother. Secretary to Ireland, another brother of Mr double-damned Walpole! Secretary to the Postmaster General, Mr shit-head Walpole's shag-wit brother-in-law!'

Louisa   I told you, it doesn't matter, I'm just a worn out old jade.

Harry   It's disease at the heart of the state!

William   No, Louisa, sweetheart, sweetheart, you're much more than that.

Harry He's like a man who poisons a fountain from which everyone must drink!

William Just ignore him, maybe he'll go away.

Harry Are you all deaf? Are you all blind? Or do you just choose not to look?

Louisa Will – is it true you put me in a set of drawings?

William (*defensive*) Everyone always thinks it's *them* I've used for a model.

Louisa I have no illusions. I only wondered. What could I do about it if you had?

William I want you to do what you know that I like.

Louisa I'm right at the bottom and on the way down.

William Fart for me. Go on, Lou. Fart in my face, Lou. Please.

Louisa Oh, Willy . . .

With a sigh **Louisa** *lifts her skirt and* **William** *disappears underneath. He is completely hidden. The parade floods onto the stage.* **Louisa** *stares straight ahead, sad, unseeing.*

Harry It's so dark . . . So bleak . . . How long till dawn?

Harry *slumps.* **Oliver,** *with bottle in hand, approaches* **Louisa.** *He squeezes her breast. She does not respond.*

Frank Look at him, he's on the go again already, the dog, and barely an hour since we left your house.

Needham I had to get him away, Frank. He was killing her. The Viscount's underclothes are caked with blood.

Oliver (*leaves* **Louisa**) Slack like a fish washed up on the beach. Not sure if one can be bothered.

Drummer Performance begins in fifteen minutes! Good seats still to be had!

They all prepare to move off. The **Man** *in the mask beckons* **Frank** *aside, away from* **Harry.**

Man Frank? 'Tis Frank, isn't it? – A word with you.

The man lowers his mask. It is **Walpole. Frank** *is stunned and frightened.*

Frank Sir . . . ! Christ.

Louisa *senses something.*

Louisa What's that?

A noise of howling wind. They all look around, uncertain.

Needham Where?

*Suddenly **Sarah** passes through them at great speed, skipping, dancing across the stage, her knife flashing close to throats and wrists and genitals, a manic Samurai in rags. As quickly as she came, she is gone. A stunned pause. A blackout. Then **Mrs Needham** screams.*

Scene V

*The **Hogarths'** house. A large bed. Moonlight coming through a window. Flickering shadows from candles in corners. **Jane** is in her nightclothes, brushing her hair.*

Jane Listen, my hair crackles with desire. Why don't you come home? William? I would do now what you wanted in the park. I just must be private, it is my nature. Under my sheets I will do anything, nothing's too dirty for my little man. He will come a million times. His heart will burst from coming.

She looks out of the window.

This is all assuming he gets home within the next five minutes, because otherwise, forget it, I'm not that devoted to the idea.

She gets into bed and blows out her candle.

His hands! I can't rid my thoughts of his hands. Stubby fingers exploring the bones in my back, grimy nails that rasp on silk, slipping, sliding, tumbling down my grassy slopes : . . We lie for hours, twined like rope, like vines, all licks and dribbles, tooth on grape, inner thigh –

*Silent and unseen, **Sarah** enters, and listens.*

– on inner thigh, he calls it the Line of Beauty, perpetual spiral of perfect art – we lose our limbs, begin to blend – we become snakes, we slither together – our flicking tongues – oh William –

Sarah *knocks against something.* **Jane** *sits up.*

Will? What are you –

Sarah *leaps on to the bed and puts the knife to* **Jane** *'s throat.*

Sarah It's a cheese knife. Recognise it? I fancy it come from your kitchen. Not a murmur now or I take the rind off you. I gather from your whimpering that Willy is not home yet . . . ? Then I shall have to wait, shan't I.

Jane What do you want? Money? I deal with the money in this house.

Sarah No, I don't want your money, what would I want with money? Unlike every other beggar in the world, I can not be purchased. My name is Sarah Sprackling. (**Jane** *gasps.*) Oh good, someone's heard of me. Your husband came to see me in my cell, down in the sump of human sewage, promising to do my picture.

Jane Didn't he do it?

Sarah Oh, he done it –

Jane He keeps his word.

Sarah – but I don't like it.

Jane Ah.

Sarah I want it back. And if he won't give it I'll kill him.

Jane Do you think that will be absolutely necessary?

A commotion outside in the hallway. The voices of **Robert Walpole** *and a* **Servant**.

Servant (*off*) No, sir, you can't go in there, that's my lady's bedroom!

Walpole (*off*) I goes where I damn well wants.

Sarah (*knife*) Hide me.

Jane Under the blankets! There's nowhere else.

Walpole (*off*) Matter of state security, this is.

Sarah *hides in the bed next to* **Jane**. **Walpole** *blusters in.* **Jane** *pretends to be waking up.*

Jane Oh, what a horrid dream . . .

Walpole Mrs Hogarth? Is that you?

Jane Who is it?

Walpole My name is Robert Walpole. Please forgive the indiscretion.

Jane Mr Walpole!

Walpole I must speak to your husband. Where is he?

Jane I don't know. Is he in trouble?

Walpole He will be if he's not careful. You know this prostitute thing? This 'Harlot's Progress'?

Jane Well what do you think? It is on easels in the drawing room.

Walpole There is a rumour, madam, there is a nasty little worm of a rumour wriggling through town. It slithered up to me only this evening, and whispered, through a mouth of slime, that William's planning a follow-up – based on me.

Jane 'Sir Robert Walpole's Progress'?

Walpole It doesn't have that ring, does it, that poetry, it lacks a certain something, do try and put him off. Mrs Hogarth, your husband is a genius. But he is no politician. He is like a child out there in the big world, away from his brush and palette. And I am very conscious of my somewhat battered public image. After all he is beholden to me, on account of the Salver.

Jane Salver? What Salver?

Walpole Hasn't he told you of the bond between us?

Jane He's always said he was an independent artist!

Walpole There is no such thing. Madam, a history lesson, very brief. Perhaps you know that on the demise of the monarch the Great Seal of England has to be redesigned, and it is the honour and duty of the Chancellor of the Exchequer, who by some accident, at the sad death of His Majesty George the First, happened to be me, to convert the old matrix into a memorial silver plate. Now Chancellors of the Exchequer do not as a rule survive the turmoil of an incoming reign, having usually made a fiscal bollocks of the preceding one, but by some fluke it chanced to be me who took delivery of His Majesty George the Second's spanking brand new Seal. Then I sets about getting an engraver for me plate.

Jane A silver engraver.

Walpole Oh, you've a sharp mind for a woman in her nightie.

Some vicious satires he had done. The Royal Family scorned! You have no idea how the laughter of the illiterate rings in the halls of St James's. Put your satires in books, by all means, 'Gulliver's Travels', yes yes yes, the Queen enjoys a read – but pictures? Everyone will get it! Worse than bloody plays! Can you imagine – a picture in every home? Your hubby-to-be was sailing into danger. I could hardly allow such influence to rest in the hands of an *artist*. I had to help him to the safe high ground of creative endeavour – the oil painting. But how to bung him up there without denting his pride? Blinding flash of inspiration, commissioned him to engrave the Walpole Salver. Lovely job he did, too, old Hercules putting the allegorical screws on Calumny and Envy. A charming introduction into the bosom of polite society, and with it the opportunity to make enough to marry. Always chuffed to help a genius earn a shilling. But he is my man now, and damned if I let him forget it.

There is a burst of angry laughter from beneath the bedclothes. **Walpole** *pulls them back to discover* **Sarah**.

And now I am embarrassed. I thought it might have been the genius. In hiding. Wrath of the gods et cetera et cetera.

Jane My friend is keeping me company whilst my husband is out.

Walpole And devilishly pleasant company, too, if a wee bit of an urchin.

Jane The noise in the hallway . . . she snuggled down . . . I will give my husband your message, Mr Walpole. If that is all? We are very tired.

Walpole Yes. No. (*He drops a purse on the bed.*) Twenty guineas. If you – do it. Now. In front of me. I burn with curiosity, it is something I have always desired to watch. How exactly do you manage to –

Jane How dare you! Please leave at once.

Walpole Very well. Pity.

Walpole *picks up his money and turns to leave.* **Sarah** *takes* **Jane**'s *chin in her hand and plants a long, hard kiss on her mouth.* **Walpole** *gapes. He takes the money from his pocket again. But when he does so,* **Sarah** *abruptly breaks off the kiss and shouts at him.*

Sarah What do you think we are?

Walpole A brace of bitches. (*He pockets his money and exits.*)

Sarah   More money than I ever seen . . . But they would make bed just like gaol. Have you ever noticed how they love the thought of women having women, but hate to think of men seducing men?

Jane   That was the Prime Minister that you just made a fool of.

Sarah   Well? Who's he going to tell? The Queen?

They fall into a fit of giggles, unable to contain themselves, letting out their tension. Then **Jane** *stops laughing.*

Jane   What do you want here? Why don't you just go away and leave us in peace?

A distant bell tolls midnight.

Sarah   This is the start of my last day on earth. Why should I leave you in peace?

Her knife-blade glints in the moonlight. Slow fade.

Act Two

Scene VI

Drury Lane, the same night. A dog barks in the distance. **William** *stands wrapped in a white sheet in the middle of the road.*

William I don't *feel* powerful. Naked like this. I don't feel like a bloke who takes advantage. Look at me, I stand here in a state of . . . droop. Authority has been sucked and squirted from me like the juice from a spanish orange. How can I be a tyrant? I am a deliberate weakling. My little foot is on nobody's throat! Look!

Louisa appears at a window above, half-dresssed.

Louisa You're a bastard, you're all bastards.

William Men will be bastards, granted, yes, the evidence is overwhelming, but I'm sorry I refuse to accept complicity in every bloody crime of the sex. I am trying hard to rise above it. I have the greatest respect for womankind. I simply happen to have come out without any bloody money.

Louisa You are an exploitative bastard, Will! Like all men you try and turn every defeat to your own advantage.

William Oh, do me a favour! It's you! You, wanting payment for a thing that should be free. Simple human loving, and you present me with a bill. Christ, the avarice of this city . . .

Louisa You can't accept your imperfection, so you unload it on to me. You foul and you defile me, then claim it's you that's abused. It's always the same.

William Do I have to stand here and listen to this shit?

Louisa Looks like it, doesn't it?

William Fucking cunt!

Louisa Then you turn violent. And out comes the language. It's always the same. Viciousness tempered with guilt.

William All I want is my clothes back, Louisa.

Louisa Then pay what you owe.

William Oh come on, darling, I thought we was friends.

Louisa Friends! Is this any way to treat your friends?

William I only asked if I could put it on the slate.

Louisa You can put it on the stove and boil it, chum, before you put it anywhere near me again. (*Exit.*)

William Lou! (*Pause.*) What a slag, honestly . . . A mercenary on the battlefields of desire. Wading through acres of red genitalia, breast bared, hips flying, and hand stretched out for her ruthless shilling. – O pity the poor debtors! They are the wretched of the earth.

Louisa reappears above. He doesn't see her.

All this for a moment's peace, in her, one second of perfection, one fleeting glimpse of beauty, when the universe drops its knickers and puts everything on view . . . simple, simple, it's all so simple . . . Then back comes chaos crashing in. Back to the body and the bartering for warmth. Thinking, does she see this apparition too – or is she, as seems highly likely, conning?

Louisa You are so self-important, William Hogarth, so puffed up, I don't know how you survive the sheer ordinariness of life, never mind draw it. 'One second of perfection'! Talk about seeing things from a male point of view! You have to learn not to piss on your mates. You can't just use people for your own purposes and then abandon them.

William I never abandoned no one. – I've come back, haven't I?

Louisa You drive me round the twist, you do! You drive me bloody barmy! I should have shopped you to your pure-arsed wife.

William Yeh, all right, but what about my clothes?

Louisa Might get a few bob for them, I suppose. I don't want you to freeze to death, however –

William You're right, it's bitter, open the door.

Louisa – so you can have this back, it's no fucking use to me.

She throws his wig out. It wafts to the ground. **William** *puts it on his head and strides about, huffing.*

William Oh, thank you very much, my precious! Thank you very, very much! At least now I can walk the streets with dignity! At least I won't be taken for a twat!

Louisa Good night. (*Exit.*)

William *seethes. Then he sniffs and wipes his nose on the sheet. Then he seethes again.*

William I have a sword, you know. Gentleman of leisure I may not be but I have bought myself a blade – saved for it for bloody years and never used the fucker! Shall I try it on your flaccid skin for sharpness?

Unseen, **Harry** *enters, drunk, with bottle. He watches* **William** *from a distance.*

Yes I like the thought! I shall chamfer my initials on your droopy old tits, and on your bum engrave the crosshatch of my vengeance! You have gone too bloody far my girl.

He turns to leave and sees **Harry**.

Wotcher, Harry.

Harry Hello, Will.

William Yes, well . . .

Harry You wouldn't, would you?

William What?

Harry All that carving and slashing.

William (*jaw thrust out*) I might.

Harry Seriously?

William I might!

Harry Why?

William She done me a mischief.

Harry I see. Well, we've all got it in us.

William She nicked my clothes!

Harry And for that, you want to cut her up?

William Fucking do, mate. Fucking make me feel a fucking lot better.

Pause. **Harry** *watches him. He breaks.*

Of course I don't, she's a friend of mine, what do you think I am, a maniac?

Harry Why'd you say it then?

William I didn't bloody mean it, did I!

Harry . . . It's easy to over-react. After you've hired a woman. One wrong word and you could kill. You've been turfed out, have you?

William All because I forgot to bring my money with me. I ask you.

Harry Will, you have never been known to forget your money. The precise whereabouts and condition of your purse is invariably the thought uppermost in your mind.

William Yes, well, thing is, I'm skint.

Harry Then why go to a tart? It's asking for trouble.

William . . . I'm in love.

Harry How does it feel?

William It hurts.

Harry The heart will ache, it is traditional.

William Not the heart. My balls.

Harry Have you tried explaining your feelings to the object of your affections? (*He indicates the house behind.*)

William What? – No, no, no, I'm not in love with her! She's a prostitute! Christ!

Harry Then who – ?

William Why, I'm in love with my wife, of course!

Harry Sorry, my mistake.

William I fucking worship her, Harry. She is my life. The blood in my veins.

Harry Forgive my abject stupidity, will you, it is the alcohol has paralysed my brains, but just tell me why in that case you come down Drury Lane of a midnight?

William I want my wife to respect me. I have these . . . impulses, you see, and I – oh, fuck, what's it got to do with you? (*He turns away. He turns back.*) Jane has certain expectations of me, right? Naturally I want to live up to them.

Harry But you sometimes need a break from being perfect.

William Yes! Need relief. Any man would.

Harry And, er –

William Louisa, yes –

Harry Does a very good job I bet.

William Hmm. – Here, how did you get on at Mrs Needham's?

Harry I don't want to talk about it. Change the subject.

Pause. They sit drinking in the gutter. Suddenly **Harry** *breaks down.*

Oh, Will, the bad taste of this town . . .

William It's as old as the wind. The disappointment after.

Harry It's not disappointment, I was not disappointed! But how could I enjoy it? I, a man of letters? A poet, dipped in that pot of flesh? Oh I got so angry with myself! The things I made the creature do . . . The worst of it all was she took it all for normal. Peggy. My bollocks adrift in her oceans of fat . . . Her weak eyes blank like bedsheets . . . .

William Don't get upset.

Harry Always been in love before. Always been passionate. Union of spirits. This was like coming in a corpse.

William Harry, it's not important.

Harry (*snuffles*) To me it is, I think it's important to admit, to recognise, what we are capable of. Because it's so alarming.

William Look, will you please not cry, I can't stand to see a man cry. It's a tough old life I know, but . . . (*Gently.*) Harry . . .

William *tries to comfort* **Harry** *without actually touching him. He offers him the bottle.*

Harry We alter the world around us but we never change ourselves inside. We hear the first rumbles of industrial progress but what will it bring us? Will it make us happy? Or will we sink deeper and deeper into the web of our own stupidity? Look at the people we allow to govern us, for God's sake! Are they working for the common good?

William Well, nobody's perfect.

Harry But you can't just leave it at that!

William I love human beings for their failures. It's the only way I can live with myself.

Harry Why won't you listen to what I'm bloody saying?

William Because you go in so hard. Everything you do is an act of aggression. Art should also celebrate. Or it does not tell the truth.

Harry No, no, it should abuse, it should insult, the audience should be shocked, disturbed, and made to think again!

William Don't be a berk. They love to be shocked! They love it! They take it as proof of their own broadmindedness! It doesn't alter a bleeding thing. You have to work gently, cleverly, bit by bit . . .

Harry No, it's just that I'm not good enough. Not hard enough. A truly oppositional ideal will outrage the most unshockable of palates.

William Oh fucking hell.

Harry I have not found it. I make too many jokes. This evening they laughed and laughed. The bastards.

William . . . Well, it was a comedy, wasn't it?

Harry England in the 1730s? A comedy?

William But Christ, if it's *funny* –

Harry Well of course it's funny, you've got to mock or you might as well curl up and die! But satire is too sugary, too easy to swallow. I dream of writing something where the laughs turn into tears. Where the wit is sharp like a mouthful of lemon. The truth is not a joke. It's dark. The only light is love, the only thing that redeems us, salvages us from the world we have made. And what do we do? We betray it.

William But what do you want? People to suddenly metamorphose overnight into some better kind of being?

Harry Less than a hundred years ago these same people executed the King! Never forget that. Nothing is impossible.

William But there's no point swimming against the tide! It's daft! What I'm gonna do is, I'm gonna do a set of prints that'll be dirt cheap to buy, right, I mean fuck, I don't care if you wrap your fish in them, but what I'm thinking of Harry is this: they'll infiltrate. My modern moral subjects. They'll sneak into peoples' homes – ordinary people – and creep up on to the walls and they'll hang over the bedsteads and they'll niggle. They'll take on the old prejudices and they'll worry them by the throat . . . they won't sicken, but they'll nag . . . .

Harry In an amusing sort of way.

William In an amusing sort of way.

Harry You just want the loot.

William I've gone so long without it, I do have rather a lust for the stuff.

Harry As an artist, William, you're a coward. You will not point your finger.

William To point your finger, Henry, you must first remove it from your arse. I admire what you write but you talk like a turd. The simple truth is, Walpole exists. He is power. I believe in the reality of power. It is a tangible thing. If power chooses to censor, then censor it will. He'll have you by the nuts, mate. You want to keep an eye on the little shrinkers.

Harry Don't patronise me. I thought you were ambitious.

William I am ambitious.

Harry But not for change. For yourself, but not for others. Not to bring down Walpole.

William Bring down this Walpole, up pops another Walpole.

Harry It's almost as if the satirist *needs* a sick society . . . has a vested interest in preserving it . . . so you can feed off it . . . suck its blood . . .

William I just want to survive. That is my ambition. Have another drink.

Harry No. No more drinks.

A sedan chair with drawn curtains is carried on by two chairmen. They set it down and open it up. **Walpole** *steps out.*

Walpole Mr Fielding. Mr Hogarth. In fancy dress. Shared bottle of gin. Jolly good.

William Servant sir.

Harry Sir.

Walpole So glad I've managed to find you at last, William. I have just paid a courtesy call on your charming wife. I didn't know she was a lesbian.

William She's not.

Walpole She's not, she's not, what am I saying, how could she possibly be? Married to a chap like yourself. She must just have been experimenting. We all do when we are young. But when we grow up we find we want to settle down. Oh, we do, Henry, we do. We discover that what we want most, what gives us the greatest pleasure and the greatest freedom to enjoy it, is stability. The ship of state on an even keel. No danger to the cargo. Oh, heaving and rolling with the natural swell, perhaps, but the captain in full command. By some strange quirk of fate I have ended up at the helm, lashed to the wheel of this glorious boat. And I have steered her on to a course of peace and prosperity. Because peace is the perfect condition for trade, and trade will make us rich, and rich is what we want to be, correct? Fifty thousand men slain this year on the fields of Europe, and not one of them English! How proud I am of that. (*Pause.*) Or would you prefer a hunting metaphor? Gentlemen? I am a hunting man. Across the stubbly fields of Norfolk, I hunt, foxes or women, don't mind which. Backside raw in the saddle, horse at a furious gallop, naked lady making for the woods, my idea of heaven. However it would be positively no trouble at all to me to set my hounds on the scent of meddlesome artists. Wherever you go, into what ditch, behind what copse, through what fields of swaying barely I will hunt you down and dip my finger in your blood and smear it in triumph on the nearest child's face. (*To* **Harry**.) Metaphorically speaking, of course, this is all part of the same extended conceit, as I'm sure you recognise. I have some literary aspirations myself, you see.

Harry I wouldn't count on overnight success if I were you.

Walpole Success may not be what I'm after, boy. – I believe it will one day become the mark of a cultured society, that its artistic members realise when they have gone too far, and voluntarily apply the curb. It is a struggle, self-restraint, dear me yes – but think of the rewards.

Harry What are they exactly?

Walpole Well, I shan't have to raid your theatre and charge all the actors under the vagrancy laws, as I did shortly after the final curtain this evening.

Harry Oh, not again! Why?

Walpole The play was offensive. Public sensibilities were offended.

Harry How do you know? You weren't even there!

Walpole I will pass over the unkind satirical jibes at myself, for the age cries out for satire, they say. Which must mean the age is pretty damn sure of itself. But I hear, sir, that you are preparing yet another scurrilous item.

Harry It's going to be called 'The Historical Register' – a political calendar of the year – all four seasons of your mould and decay.

Walpole Don't proceed with it. Or I shall be forced to introduce a censor's office.

Harry You can't.

Walpole I was thinking of giving the job to the Lord Chamberlain.

Harry You can't!

William Don't push your luck, mate.

Harry Parliament will never approve it!

Walpole Shut up. (*To* **William**.) You're toying with the idea of another Progress series, are you?

William I think you must be misinformed.

Walpole Good, I don't like progress, I like things as they are.

Harry I should like to know your constitutional –

Walpole Will you be quiet.

Harry This is a free country, sir! I am a freeborn Englishman, and I have a right to speak!

Walpole Oh, do grow up, Henry.

Harry Go on, then! Do it! Do it, if you dare!

Walpole You've gone all red.

Harry I was just thinking, when you burn your boats, what a bloody good fire it makes! (*Exit, angrily.*)

William (*defending* **Harry**) He's had a bad day.

Walpole Why? The play was a triumph. Why are you chaps so perverse? (*Pause. He sits and drinks from the gin bottle.*) My houses are stuffed full of art, you know. It's such a damned good investment. I got a Titian last year for two pounds ten. It's already worth double that. I love art, I love it more than all my other property, they're so neat and compact, those rectangles of wealth. But you have to win through to posterity, William, or you are worth nothing. You have to exist in the future, and for that you have to function in the present. I believe you have a yearning for an amendment to the Copyright Act. To apply it to the visual arts.

William . . . If I am to live.

Walpole See what I can do. Are you going home to Janey looking like that? – I'm not surprised she's bent.

Walpole *gets back into his sedan chair and is carried off.* **William** *wraps the sheet tightly about him. He clutches at his head. Pause. The sedan chair returns. It is set down in front of him. Nothing happens.*

William Was there something we forgot?

The chair opens and out steps **Louisa.** *She is in tattered rags, and ravaged by an indescribably disgusting disease. The flesh hangs off her in strips. Her face is horribly disfigured. Her hands drip green slime.*

Louisa Yes, Willy, we forgot about the pox, didn't we?

William (*in terror*) Louisa!

William *tries to run but, as in a dream, his feet are like lead.* **Louisa** *reaches a slimy hand under his sheet and grabs his private parts. Blackout.*

Scene VII

An apartment in a palace. A large, ornate bed. A woman lies in it. **Walpole**, *half-dressed, sits at a nearby table, writing. He screws up a sheet of paper and throws it away.*

Walpole It's not as easy as I thought. The costume changes are a bugger. I need the heroine half-naked for the climax, so I've got to find a reason to get her off-stage and then I've got to find another reason to get her on-stage again. Give me the House of Commons any day. (*He looks to the woman.*) I know it won't be a popular law. But hang me a booming economy seems to breed subversion more than an age of hardship. It is precisely the popularity of the playhouses that renders them such a threat. Oh, I long to bring in a sensible, modern system, in which it is simply made plain to these chaps that it's in their own interests to toe the Lord Chamberlain's line . . . A hint here . . . A whisper there . . . Get the Artistic Director in for a cup of tea, wave a small cheque in his face . . . Just nudge the idea in. Where did the thinking spring from, that art must necessarily equal trouble? I am pacific, it is my nature, I believe with all my heart that what we need for the growth of the nation is peace. I don't like trouble and nor do the people. We like a quiet life and a decent dinner and why can't these toe-rags accept it? – Ah! Good! (*He writes fast.*) Get your costume off, you difficult old bag.

The woman in the bed is **Queen Caroline.**

Queen (*German accent*) I do not remember saying you could get up and work.

Walpole Oh, I thought we had done.

Queen Undress.

Walpole It's a critical scene!

Queen Undress!

Walpole Yes, your Majesty.

Queen We don't approve of censoring the peoples' entertainment. It's not the kind of thing we're used to in this country. It seems not to accord with our sense of what is England.

Walpole It won't be censorship, not outright censorship, I'd never get anyone to vote for that – just a system of licensing, a regulating hand on the temperamental shoulder. The actual dirty work of censoring will be done by the artists themselves. That's the beauty of it.

Queen So every play must get a licence. Then can they be performed?

Walpole But of course! If they can get a licence.

Queen Might I suggest, Minister, that this proposal of yours contains an element of – malice?

Walpole History's built on the lowest of motives.

Queen And every man has his price. I know your pet remarks. You are taking an unconscionably long time with your trousers. When we give a royal command we expect you to perform. Quick!

Walpole Yes, your Majesty. I'm hurrying up.

Queen I want to gaze upon your flesh, your flabby, blotchy flesh, your sinews, the slack pink muscle of government.

Walpole It is not something I normally shows to the world, ma'am.

Queen It is not elegant. Not beautiful. Not art.

Walpole I can go if the mood has left you –

Queen I fully intend to take my pleasure. To see the user used.

Walpole Caroline . . .

Queen What your political opponents are saying, of course, is that the time is ripe for expansion, we have the wealth, we have the resources, the army and the navy, we could thrust across the globe in the search for brand-new markets. Our merchant class has aspirations, Robin. There is a spirit of adventure in the land, I smell it. It hints that you are finished. Unless someone protects you.

Walpole Your Majesty's nostril is ever acute. But what about the King?

Queen I am the reign. Through my husband I exercise power. Let him march up and down with his soldiers. That leaves me free to concentrate on more important matters, such as the religious life of the state. As you may have observed, the people are morally lax. We need some tough new bishops.

Walpole Oh, we do, we do.

Queen I wish to appoint one. Robertson.

Walpole What!

Queen An excellent man. High church but with rationalist tendencies.

Walpole I know a better bet for a mitre – a chaplain who's demonstrated that the plays of our times offend against fourteen hundred texts in the Bible.

Queen Don't try to manipulate *me*. I have discussed the calculus with Leibnitz and astronomy with Newton. I am concerned with serious theology, not the sad boasts of the village idiot.

Walpole But Robertson will vote against me in the Lords! The balance of power will be upset!

Queen (*a smile*) Dear me. That sounds a terribly tenuous system. How will you get your Licensing Act through?

Walpole I'm working on a scheme, don't worry. (*He indicates his writing.*)

Queen But then you will need your Royal Assent.

Walpole . . . The price of which is a Bishop, is it? This is going to cost me a fortune in the long run. For that, will you also consider a little bit of business regarding the laws of copyright, which I beg leave to introduce?

Queen All I wish you to introduce at this moment, Prime Minister, is your tongue, your big, fat, talkative tongue.

Walpole It seems only fair and logical to me that, as we legislate to clarify the ownership of all our other products, so we should do the same for art.

Queen All right, all right! But why have you still your woollens on? Did I not say naked? Naked and kneeling before your Queen?

Walpole Majesty.

Reluctantly he continues undressing.

Queen Wait. I have changed my mind. *(He groans.)* The carnal urge has suddenly left me. I think I'd sooner talk to the Archbishop. You may go.

Walpole *starts to dress.*

Go! At once! Audience over!

Walpole *(bowing)* Your humble servant, madam.

Humiliated, **Walpole** *scoops up his clothing and his papers and bows his way out. Pause. Then the* **Queen** *collapses in a fit of hysterical laughter.*

Scene VIII

A pillory. Still the same night. In the stocks stands **Mrs Needham**. *Egg, rotten fruit, and blood drip from her face.*

Needham God is good. *(Pause.)* God is just. *(Pause.)* He is, he is! Prostitution is a wicked trade, I knew he wouldn't like it. But this sinner will hang on her cross, O merciful Father, until she hears your voice call down from heaven in forgiveness, Needham, the Bawd, you have suffered enough, pucker your lips on the soles of my feet, we shall enter Jerusalem together. I wish to announce my retirement from business. I have some capital, Lord, not as much as I'd hoped for given my talents – oh, I was a goer in my time, I could take ten bob with my legs together – but that was when I freelanced. Once you become an employer your overheads hit the roof. . . . And the paperwork!

Behind her, **William** *comes on out of the dark. He still wears only sheet and wig. He creeps on furtively, shaking with cold.*

But if I survive the night, Christ Jesus, I will give my life and my savings to your mission on earth. Let me be your handmaiden, let me be your scourge in the city of sin. For I know the guilty. I can name names. You will see some blushing faces I promise you! – Who's there?

William's *behind her. She can't turn round.*

Who is it? Come where I can see you. I smell you! You reek of gin.

William *just stands there.*

Don't hurt me, don't harm me, I haven't done anything awful, but a mob of screaming puritans got hold of me tonight, priests and thin women, I don't mind, allow them their outrage, there was a wave of morality burst upon us after Mr Walpole's constables had raided that theatre. And they dragged me to the Justice and he slammed me in the stocks! And then the apprentice boys pushed stones in their rotten tomatoes, and pelted me half to death! If you would wipe my face . . . ? Be kind to me . . . ? I'm cut in a thousand places . . . by the fruit of the self-righteous . . .

William *puts a hand on her.*

Oh! Mister! Your hand on my rump . . . I have the hindquarters of a horse, haven't I? I once heard of a gentleman who said England was a paradise for women, and hell for horses. Well he can take me out for a canter any old time. Little dig in the flanks and I'm off mate. Oh, don't abuse me, don't, I feel so vulnerable, I'm dripping blood and egg-yolk, I can see it in on the ground, like a little kiddie's painting of the sun.

William, *from behind, pulls off the woman's skirt and puts it round himself.*

Don't please! I'm dry! I'll scrape! A whore can be raped, you know, just as a bankrupt can be swindled. Lord Jesus protect me . . .

William *pulls off her blouse and puts that on.*

Do I know you? Is that it? Are you someone I have had? Some complainer out of all the happy thousands, bent on getting it for nothing? Will you speak to me you pervert!

William *tries on her shoes. They fit.*

I will die of freezing . . . I'll be gone by dawn . . . But God will punish you. God will burn your lecher's eyes out. He will tear at your heart with his fingernails. God's fingernails, matey, think of that! God's rasping scratching omnipresent nails!

William, *now dressed, drapes the sheet over the woman's head, and leaves.*

Wanker! Pass by on the other side, then! Go on! Pass by! I can hear you shuffling away . . . Devil!

He is gone. Pause. Slowly her head droops.

Lord have mercy on me. Christ have mercy on me. Lord have mercy on me. Christ have mercy on me.

Fade out.

Scene IX

William's *studio. Canvasses stacked against the walls. Easels. Clutter. Enter* **Jane** , *with* **Sarah**, *who is holding a knife to her back.* **Sarah** *motions* **Jane** *to stay still. She herself wanders round looking at pictures with a great curiosity.*

Sarah Has he ever painted you?

Jane No.

Sarah Why not? It's very odd. You'd think he'd want to paint his wife. Specially if she looked as clean and nice as you do.

Jane Oh, I'm very plain.

Sarah You're prettier than me.

Jane You have more character.

Sarah But no money to pay.

Jane Well, he had a commission to do you, didn't he?

Sarah Oh? Who from?

Jane How should I know? I don't keep up with all his business dealings.

Sarah I thought you said you handled the money . . . ?

Pause. **Sarah** *finds* **William**'s *sword, hanging in its scabbard over the corner of a painting. She takes it out. She puts the knife aside. She examines the gleaming sword with pleasure.*

You gone very quiet. I kill with delight, lady. That's what I'm like. It's how I make my mark. (*Pause.*) I thought, do one intelligent thing before I die. Get my future back. I was surprised I could be moved like that. I thought I was rock, a wall of granite, I thought I was the cliff that the waves bash against but never get inside of. But suddenly I was awash with it. Indignation. Well, shite, the cheek of it, to take my face and – ! (*Pause.*) Once you've made the big decision all the others make themselves. Long time since I've seen the smoky London streets. The fug whirled and eddied round me as I ran, my feet asplash in rivulets of piss, my neck and buttocks clenched expecting knife or fist or hammer. I came the back way. Through the shadows to Covent Garden. Now tell me truly why he's never painted you.

Jane . . . I don't want to be painted.

Sarah You do.

Jane I don't! Time and again I refuse him permission. I won't let him put me in that role, the role of the subject. I am not his subject, I am his lover and his wife, and I will never let him do my portrait, I will never surrender up that kind of power.

Sarah God, I wish I had your brain.

Jane You could have, I'll tutor you, I'll discover you to yourself, only put the sword away, Sarah, will you?

Sarah You been tutoring your husband, too, from what he says.

Jane Oh? What does he say?

Sarah He says you've got him thinking like a woman now. It all went over my head, rather.

Jane I simply want to make him think about his side of the bargain. The contract of marriage.

Sarah Why?

Jane Because I want it to last, I suppose.

Sarah Why?

Jane Because I love him. For all his faults. Heaven knows why I'm telling this to you. You want to murder him.

Sarah Whatever gave you that idea? (*Pause.*) How does he expect to put the whole of me, all my doings, all my dreams and disappointments in a few small dollops of paint? He done me in a prison in a city full of smoke. That's not me. That's not how I think of me. I think of me out in the open. Flat on my back in a hayrick, beneath a mackerel sky, dreaming of all the treats I'll have when I comes up to town . . . Ambition is a curse!

Jane It's not.

Sarah A fucking bane, ambition! A noose around your neck, that constant, constant yearning for more. Look at me for an example. Product of impossible desires.

Jane Oh, don't say that. Think of what William's achieved!

Sarah . . . Tell us yours then.

Sarah *is leafing through bundles of drawings.*

Jane It's not my place to have ambition. What could I do with it if I had it? I want my husband to get on. He is my voice, through him I make my presence felt. He is the one with the power. But I can tug him in certain directions, I can tweak his pencil as it skims across the paper. I've made him think a lot harder about the way he portrays women, for example. You find me there in the pictures, my brain in his brushstrokes . . .

Sarah I couldn't do it.

Jane Why, are you too proud?

Sarah No, I ain't proud.

Jane Yes, you are, I think.

Sarah I cut and slashed my pride. I butchered it. (*Pause.*) The difference is, that you believe in a time to come. Because you love. I don't. I don't know what it's like.

Jane It's a mixture . . . of being amazed and appalled by someone. Some of his tender sentiments amaze me. Whereas some of his habits in the toilet can be truly upsetting. It's a fine balance. If you're more amazed than appalled, you're probably in love. You're also in trouble, because you can be –

Sarah Used.

Jane Yes. Luckily William's too naive to sense when he might have me under his thumb.

Sarah I've got a feeling you ought to have a look at these.

Sarah *shows* **Jane** *a series of drawings.*

Jane Ugh, disgusting!

Sarah Mucky, yes.

Jane That's pornographic!

Sarah That's you.

Jane What?

Sarah That's you, that's a drawing of you. With a man's knob in your mouth.

Jane And another in –

Sarah He's got an imagination, hasn't he?

Jane Oh God!

Sarah He's done your portrait a hundred times.

Jane (*for the first time her composure cracks*) Oh my God! I'm going to be sick. – No I'm not, I'm going to kill him. Is that what he would like me to do? Look there is pain on my face! My lover dreams of me degraded! Ugh! Look at that! And that! And that! Horrible, horrible man!

She tears up the drawings, ripping at them in fury, stamping on them, flinging them round the room. **Sarah** *watches calmly.* **Jane** *eventually quietens down.*

How sad his life must be.

Scene X

William *makes his way through London, dressed in skirt, blouse, high-heeled shoes and wig. From the shadows comes a low wolf-whistle.* **William** *stops, frightened. From another corner comes a man's laugh.*

William *picks up his skirts and runs.*

Scene XI

The studio. **William** *enters.*

William Made it. Christ what a night.

He gets a drink, sits in his favourite chair and shuts his eyes. **Sarah** *emerges from hiding and stands in front of him, holding the sword. He sees her.*

Oh, fuck! Don't you ever give up? And that's my sword! (*An explanation comes to him.*) I'm asleep. It's all right. (*He sits down again.*)

Sarah I broke out of prison.

William (*unimpressed*) Well done.

Sarah I come for my picture.

William Don't be a berk, I'm not handing over valuable pictures to a wisp of bleeding ectoplasm, am I.

Sarah *pricks him with the sword.*

Bitch! You're real! Christ!

Jane *emerges from a hiding place.*

Jane Yes, William, she is completely real.

William Jane!

Jane (*stares at him*) Why are you dressed like that?

William . . . I've suddenly gone very muzzy in the head, perhaps I better go and have a lie down.

Sarah (*sword*) Stay there!

William (*to* **Sarah**) You keep out of this, it's purely domestic, this. (*To* **Jane**.) It's a practical joke.

Jane You rotten lying pig!

William Please, please don't be difficult, darling, I've had such a terrible day.

Jane Why not? Why not be difficult?

Sarah Chop his knackers off.

William Oh, leave it out.

Jane Where have you been, then?

William . . . I was with the lads, I ran into some of the lads, and I'd forgotten it was the first night of Harry's play, and they dragged me along and I admit we had one or two beers, I'm not perfect, I have my weak points and the booze is one of them, yes, anyway it was a huge success you ask anybody and we all ended up in the actresses' dressing-room, Harry insisted we all went backstage, because there was a – bit of a party, and I was prevailed upon to do a comic turn in female attire, that's another thing I've not told you about but Jane we haven't been married that long, I'm renowned for this number I do in a frock, and then do you know what? The theatre was raided by Walpole's men and you don't believe a bloody word of this do you?

Sarah We found your drawings.

William Drawings, what drawings, the place is full of drawings – ?

Jane Drawings of me.

William I've never done a drawing of you, you don't allow it! (*Pause.*) Ah. Those drawings.

Jane Well? What have you got to say about them?

William . . . I think I got the proportions of your legs all wrong, but then I was working from –

Jane I hate you!

Sarah Chop his nuts off, I say.

William No!

Jane But those pictures, Will!

William I'm sorry!

Jane Of me in the sexual act!

William God I'm sorry, I don't know what got into me, I'm very very sorry.

Jane Not good enough!

William Jane . . .!

Jane Not good enough! Not nearly! I devote my life to you. And how do you repay me? With ridicule and filth. I had somehow got this cranky notion that you were a sensitive man. But you're not, are you, you're just ordinary, this is what saddens me, you're just like all the rest!

William Who says? What bum-hole smears my honour?

Jane Sir Robert Walpole. Told us a tale. About a silver plate.

William Ah . . . well . . . Have faith in me, Janey, I may have done some daft things, but sweetheart, it's the same old Will under all his baggage.

Jane That's what I'm worried about. Whatever possessed you to do those awful drawings?

William Look, it's the pressure, that's what it is . . . I sit at my table and I fiddle with my charcoal and my mind is off and away, I don't even realise I'm doing it, there are nightmare things that I have got caged up, hairy, growling, they scrabble at the skin of me, and sometimes slither out. Have you noticed there is that quality of horror in even my gentlest work? How did it get there? What is there in me that I cannot seem to tame? I'm quite a nice bloke really! I'm only trying to make my way in the world. And I do it all for you. Everything, for you.

Jane (*softly*) You silly little fool, why do you always have to learn the hard way? Fail! For heaven's sake, fail! Be a disaster! Be a pauper! I wouldn't love you any the less.

They gaze into each others' eyes. **Sarah**, *whose presence they have forgotten, slips the sword up under* **William**'s *skirt. He stands on tiptoe.*

Sarah (*quietly*) Listen you pair of lovebirds, I want my pissing shitting picture back and by fuck I want it now.

William . . . I'm afraid I've got some rather bad news.

Sarah What?

William I ain't got it.

Jane Where is it?

William I dropped it off at the printer's.

Sarah We'll go and get it.

William He'll be closed.

Sarah We'll get the key.

William I don't know where he lives, I'm sorry!

Sarah Why did you take it to a printer's?

William Oh, I've got someone working on the plate.

Sarah What's the plate?

William To make the copies.

Sarah Copies . . .? One picture, I thought, One painting, to hang in a rich man's study, and stare down relentless with loathing and hate, a curse on every generation! But no, not good enough for Mr Up-to-the-minute, you'd have me printed on a thousand sheets of paper, clogging up the gutters, plugging cracks in tavern walls, eat and sleep and crapped on, by them that think they're good . . . ? And I'll be on sale at me execution, will I, with me last words in print before I've said 'em?

William I am an artist. I exist to put the world in pictures.

Sarah Well you're not putting me. Come on, we're off to this printer's.

William We can't get in!

Sarah We'll kick down the door!

William One small problem. I never went to the printer's.

Jane You never went to the theatre, either, did you?

William No, I . . . We . . . We went to a gambling club.

Jane Oh, William!

William I gambled away my money, my clothes – and your picture.

Sarah Oh, shite! Who to?

William A man I didn't know – with a long hooked nose and a limp.

Sarah You are fucking lying, aren't you! Right!

William I think I'll be able to win it back tomorrow, I'm feeling very lucky!

Jane Don't hurt him, Sarah, please!

Sarah *raises the sword to strike* **William**. *He dodges away.* **Jane** *tries to hold* **Sarah***'s arm. At that moment* **Louisa** *enters, with a crash.*

William Lou! What do you want?

Louisa I changed my mind.

She throws his clothes down in the middle of the room.

Sarah Who are you?

Jane She's a common prostitute.

William – Who does a bit of laundry on the side!

Jane Is that where you've spent the evening? Up this woman's skirts?

William Wait! Give me a chance to think!

Sarah Why've you come here?

Louisa I was invited.

Jane No you weren't.

Louisa My turn, I thought, to paint a picture. A very private portrait. Of Willy and his ways.

William Oh, no.

Sarah What, has he done you too?

Louisa I can't be sure, I never seen them. – You robbing him, are you?

Sarah No, he's robbing me.

Louisa Up and up he goes. I watch from in the gutter. Daubing paint on canvas with his fingers like a kid smearing shit on walls. And they buy it! They pay money for it! In the salons and soirées of the West End, they dip into the hot-pot of his brains, and what do they find? Pictures of a prostitute. Dying of the clap.

Jane He's just a man. You have to make allowances.

Louisa Fine, in that case I can tell you how he likes to lie down on the floor and have me stand over him heaving and straining and –

Jane Stop it! Stop it! Why are you doing this?

Louisa Because I loved him. Once.

Jane (*shock*) You? Why?

Louisa Well – why do you?

William (*glum*) Why does anybody?

Sarah Belt up.

Jane Be quiet.

Louisa Shut your fucking trap.

William With a bit of luck I'm imagining all this.

Louisa But can you distinguish any more? Between pencil lines and people? You pin us like moths to your paper and you sit and watch us squirm.

Sarah That's right, he does, that's right.

Louisa I'm finished, Will. I'm all wore out. Unsellable. Just wanted you to see.

Sarah I know how you feel. He done one of me and all.

Jane (*to* **Louisa**) Please go. I think you've said enough.

Sarah Fucking shut up, you, we're talking about art.

Louisa (*to* **Jane**) How can you stick with him? Despite everything you know?

Jane He is my husband. He loves me.

Louisa What makes you think he won't betray you? To get another step up that bleeding ladder he's got lodged in his head?

Sarah (*to* **Louisa**) Tell me how he done you, the composition and that.

Louisa (*to* **Jane**) We drag ourselves down, do you know that, not him, not anyone, *us*. Love? I shit on love. Daily.

Sarah (*urgent*) Tell me how he done you!

Louisa (*weary*) What difference does it make?

Sarah He sat me at a table. In a beam of light from the window. The shadows falling on the filth and straw. He were going to put my gaoler in but then he said he wouldn't. Good job too 'cause I've killed him. (*Laughs.*) Wouldn't look too bright, would it? Picture of me in a prison cell I've just escaped from being guarded by a bloke I've just done up.

Louisa Oh my God . . . You're Sarah Sprackling, are you?

Sarah That's right.

Louisa Then – this is meant to be you?

Louisa *produces the sketch of* **Sarah** *and unrolls it.*

Sarah Me picture!

Louisa I've been staring and staring, thinking . . . how does she feel?

Sarah Give it!

William No!

Sarah I said give it!

William Don't, Lou, please!

Jane Look out!

Sarah lunges for the picture and spears it on the point of her sword.

Sarah Now I have you, I have you at last. My little darling. Now I have a hold of you. Tried to go off on your own din't you? Tried to give me the slip.

She holds the paper to a candle flame.

Oh, doesn't that look pretty. That pretty blushing face. Burn you whore! And don't never desert me again.

The picture burns.

I got this fantastical feeling running up and down my backbone like a ball of lightning, whoosh. Quiver of sleeping flesh come suddenly to life. I set out to do a thing and I done it. What a fucking wonderful feeling.

The picture is gone. She lays down the sword.

All done now.

Jane Then please – go.

Sarah Yes. Be dawn soon. Be time soon.

Louisa What way are you walking?

Sarah East. Back to Newgate.

Louisa To the hangman?

Sarah Coming with me? Keep me company?

Louisa Why don't you run for it? Go on, run for it, run free, take off across Islington fields and vanish . . . Sleep by day and run by night . . . Change your identity, become someone else . . .

Sarah I am just barely smart enough to be me, what chance have I got of becoming someone else?

Louisa But surely you don't want to die?

Sarah Yes, I do. Who wants to live like this?

Louisa I'm confused, I don't understand – why?

Sarah ... Tooth of a hanged person supposed to be a love potion, ain't it. Some unloved woman will pluck my yellow stumps. Grind them in some farmboy's porridge. And I hope she gets some pleasure from it, too. Little snatch of warmth in the cold time, just now, aching for the sun after the chaos of the night ... Will you do me a favour?

Louisa I might. What?

Sarah Come along the road and I'll tell you.

They go off together. **William** *grabs a piece of paper and a pencil and begins to sketch fast.*

Jane Thank God they've gone ... Trembling like a leaf ... What are you doing?

William Ssh! Sketching from memory, technical memory, got to concentrate –

Jane I beg your pardon?

William Get it down the printer's first thing in the morning.

Jane William! No! (*Snatches away his pencil.*) Let the poor woman die gracefully.

William Gracefully? You call that gracefully?

Jane She thinks it is.

William She's bonkers!

Jane William, I have to say it, I think this is immoral.

William I know that. I'm not thick.

Jane Think how she'd feel if you published her picture now!

William Christ, she'll never know!

Jane She is choosing when to die. What else has she ever chosen in her life? Perhaps that has a kind of grace. (*Pause.*) Abandon it. For me.

William (*concedes*) The world will never hear of Sarah Sprackling, she will never have existed, she will be a ghost, who stalks the landscape of my brain, how's that?

Jane Thank you. I am going back to bed now. We shall discuss all this tomorrow. (*Pause.*) The thought of you with that old whore . . .! Ugh! And Robert Walpole. You're in too deep! And oh, when I saw those vile drawings, I was livid! But then I stopped and calmed down and tried to think sensibly about it and – I began to look on you as, well, what shall we say? Cripple? Some sort of emotional cripple? Not got the use of all your bits. And all I can feel for one of those is pity. Goodnight. (*Exit.*)

William Night night, sweetheart.

Immediately, from another entrance, a **Stage-hand** *enters, crosses the stage, gives* **William** *a polaroid camera, and exits.*

Oh. Thanks.

William *examines the camera with great interest. Immediately* **Jane** *returns.* **William** *guiltily hides the camera behind his back.*

Jane And don't have any more to drink tonight, William, or you will ruin your health. (*Exit.*)

Immediately **Oliver** *appears from another entrance, looking thoroughly debauched. He advances on* **William** *from behind, seeing only the costume. He grabs at* **William**'s *bum.*

Oliver My dear! I came.

William (*turns*) Oliver!

Oliver Oh, bother, it's you, is it? I thought I'd find Janey here alone.

William What?

Oliver I will not be hobbled by convention, it's so very dreary, don't you think? I spend my nights up a lot of loose streetgirls, but it's no good, I don't come off. I need a female of good breeding. Your wife will do. Is that all right?

William Er . . .

Oliver One has to do what gives one pleasure, William. The world may end tomorrow. Pop. Then what are you left with?

William That's not a bad argument. Here, do you know how to work one of these?

Oliver Yes, you look through here, push this, and –

A flash. **Oliver** *takes a photo of* **William**. *The picture ejects itself.* **William** *takes the camera back and stares at the photograph. It's blank, of course.*

William Hmm, well I don't think much of that.

Jane *enters, seductively dressed.*

Wait a minute . . .!

The picture starts to come up. **William** *stares at it.* **Jane** *embraces* **Oliver**, *and leads him aside. They make love. She calls out to her husband.*

Jane William. William.

William *sees them now, and starts to take photographs of them.* **Harry** *enters.*

Harry Hello, Will.

William Wotcher, Harry.

Harry *kisses* **William** *passionately on the mouth.* **William** *is surprised, but doesn't resist.* **Walpole** *enters.*

Walpole (*stern*) William . . .

William I'm a bit involved at the moment. With my friend.

Walpole *produces a knife and sticks it in* **Harry**'s *back.* **Harry** *dies.*

William *jumps away.*

Now look what you've done!

Walpole It's all right, I'll get away with it.

Walpole *goes towards* **Oliver** *and* **Jane**. **Harry** *sits up.* **William** *yelps.* **Walpole** *turns.* **Harry** *blows a raspberry at* **Walpole**. **Walpole** *blows a bigger raspberry at* **Harry**. **Walpole** *goes to* **Jane** *and joins in.* **Frank** *enters with a mouthful of money. He spits the money at* **William** .

Frank My turn.

Frank *goes to* **Jane** *and joins in.*

Harry And mine.

Harry *goes to* **Jane** *and joins in.* **William** *photographs the proceedings.*

William Christ, this is good. Jane, I'm disgusted with you. What a slut. I'm appalled! Four at once! Bloody hell. – Here, lift your leg a fraction.

Photographs rain from the camera. **Jane** *jumps up, runs back and points at* **William** .

Jane Now! Get him! Get him good!

The **Drummer** *enters, playing a pounding beat.* **Jane** *exits. The four men advance on* **William** .

William Oh no . . .

They chase him and strip him of his clothes. He tries to scrabble away but he is surrounded. The drumbeat drives into his brain. Each of the men produces a camera, all with flash.

Walpole Now! Take his picture! Take his picture! Put him in the file! Put him in the file!

They all photograph a naked and terrified man crouching on the floor.

William Jane! Janey! Janey! Janey! Janey! Jan-ey!

Jane *enters, now restored to her normal demure self, and dressed once again in her nightclothes, yawning.*

Immediately all the dream figures exit. All **Jane** *can see is the sobbing* **William** .

Jane Oh, Will . . . oh, darling . . . (*Takes him in her arms.*)

William Janey, it was nasty, it was you, you were doing it with Oliver and you were – nasty pictures –

Jane Now come along. I don't think you're very well, are you, darling?

She wraps him in a blanket and leads him to bed.

It's dawn. Come along with me to bed. Little boy needs a proper rest. Let's get you tucked up.

She puts him into bed. He sobs.

It's all right, cry. Cry and cry. You can't keep it all rammed down inside. You have to let people know of your feelings for them. It's vital, Will, it really is. Otherwise your work is a lie. Isn't it?

Pause. She looks out of the window.

It's starting to snow. Winter. – I'll let you paint me if you want. Do you want? I'd sooner we had it all out in the open. Paint me, I can contain it. Knowing what I know. I will not let go of you, for the sake of a little pride. (*Laughs gently.*) You and your silly dreams.

Oliver and I indeed! He is such a dreadful rake. (*Pause.*) Snow covering up everything now. All the birds will fly away. Where do they go, Will? Some unmapped land? Can you see it in your head?

She gets into bed.

I will guard you. I will guard your reputation. Sleep now. Deep down underground like a tulip bulb. Sleep now, and come up later.

She lies down and pulls the covers over their heads. Immediately **Sarah** *drops from above. dangling on the end of a rope. She swings at the foot of the bed.* **Louisa** *runs on, grabs* **Sarah**'s *legs, and pulls downwards with all her weight. Sound of the crowd roaring at the hanging. Spot on* **Louisa**, *her eyes wide with horror, and fade.*

Scene XII

Several months later, by the banks of the Thames. Low tide at a 'stairs' or landing-place at Wapping. Steps leading down from the wharf to the river. Ancient wooden beams and posts. An old boat overturned on the mudbank. **Harry** *stands on the steps. He writes on a scrap of paper. He stops writing. He is dejected.* **Frank** *and* **Oliver** *enter above, along the wharf.* **Oliver** *has the black patches on his neck and face which signify a pox. The scene starts slow and quiet.*

Frank The ice is breaking up.

Pause.

Oliver I hate spring.

Pause.

Frank We need a boat to ferry us downriver.

Oliver I hate sunshine. I hate it when the daffodils come out.

Pause.

Frank There's Harry.

Harry (*turns*) It's happened. Walpole's closed me down.

Frank Yes, we passed the Act last night, late night sitting you know.

Oliver You didn't vote for it, did you?

Frank I gave my maiden speech, against the motion.

Oliver Brave man.

Frank Then I voted for it.

Oliver Quite. So did I in the Upper House.

Harry I now have to apply to the office of the Lord Chamberlain for a license to perform any new interlude, tragedy, comedy, opera, play, farce, prologue or epilogue. Or I shall be deemed a rogue and a vagabond and punished accordingly.

Oliver That is what you wanted, is it not?

Harry But how am I supposed to make a living?

Frank Get along and apply for the blessed license. We all have to abide by the law.

William *enters, looking affluent in a new coat.*

Oliver The genius himself has come along. This is indeed an honour.

William Hullo, lads. Aren't I just a Beefsteak like the rest of you?

Frank Long time since we've seen you at a meeting.

William . . . And where are we going today?

Oliver Down the Thames to Kent. (*With distaste.*) The green fields of Kent.

Frank We have undertaken to provide the aesthetic education of an English artist. This will be your Grand Tour. The fruity air of Kent will lend you inspiration.

William What for?

Harry The art of the dung-heap.

William . . . Thought you were a bit quiet.

Harry I've seen your advertisements. In the press.

Oliver Oh, yes, bravo! Astonishment in the coffee-shops! The general view is, with this new Copyright Act, you'll become the first English painter to succeed without patronage.

Harry 'The Rake's Progress'.

William Yes?

Harry 'The Rake's Progress'.

William You don't like the title.

Harry It's just sex. You're obsessed with sex.

William Am I fuck. It's a serious work. Me and Jane spent the whole winter on it. What I'm obsessed with is beauty. The truth about beauty.

Harry There is no truth about beauty. Beauty disguises truth. It is impossible to write a beautiful play.

Frank Ignore him, Will. The Prime Minister's just shut his theatre.

Oliver He read out a play in Parliament. It's called 'The Golden Rump'.

Frank It's filthy. Mr Walpole says he got if off a theatre manager, who hinted Henry Fielding was the author.

Harry Which is quite impossible, I couldn't plot a play that amateurishly if I tried.

Beat.

Oliver There's a boat.

Frank Hey, Waterman! – There's some old biddy in it.

They go down towards the river.

William You coming?

Harry No. I've no business in Kent. I've met a very nice girl, I think I'd sooner be with her.

William Look, what's the matter with you?

Harry Nothing, absolutely nothing.

William You have to try, Harry. You have to make an effort.

Harry Why?

William God, what is the world coming to, when you can't even talk to your mates.

Harry You've done a deal, haven't you? They're calling it Hogarth's Act, do you know that? What do you have to do, Will, to get your name on the statute books? What do you have to sell?

William Well if you're going to be like that you can stick it up your arse.

William *goes to* **Frank** *and* **Oliver**.

Harry Oh, fuck . . .

William Harry ain't coming.

Oliver Oh, leave him to sulk.

William That our boat?

William *exits to the river.*

Harry Will, we're supposed to be friends, everyone thinks we're friends . . .!

But he's gone. **Mrs Needham** *enters from the river. She wears black, and carries a crucifix and a bible.*

Frank Welcome to London, madam. Christ alive it's her.

Oliver Mrs Needham. Bonjour.

Needham Good morning, boys. Off to church?

Frank We are going on a peregrination.

Needham I see. Was that Mr Hogarth I just passed, whose 'Harlot's Progress' has turned so many maidens off the downward path to hell?

Frank Yes.

Needham Thought so. Here, boatman, here's a ha'penny tip.

She lobs a coin towards the boat. But she throws badly and it falls into the mud below. She gives **Frank** *another coin.*

Oh, silly me, Lord forgive my wastefulness. My spell in the stocks, it withered my arms. Please, Frank, give the man this and tell him I will pray for his safety upon the foaming waters. Is there any act of sacrifice I can perform for either of you? Any good deed? No? (*Low voice.*) I've got a black girl in. Yes, a hottentot, a darkie, dark as your deepest thoughts. Like to try, Viscount? An extra half crown will secure it.

Oliver I've never had a black before.

Needham (*fingers his pox-marks*) Or double for the blighted.

Frank Oliver, come on.

Oliver Perhaps when I get back . . .

Frank Cast off, Will!

Exit **Frank** *and* **Oliver**. **Mrs Needham** *goes up the steps to* **Harry**.

Needham Young fellow? We're back to business as usual. Except on Sundays, I don't hold with trading on the Sabbath.

Harry *shakes his head.* **Mrs Needham** *shrugs and exits.* **Harry** *sobs. A figure emerges from under the upturned boat. It is* **Louisa**. *She is utterly filthy and decrepit. She slithers across the mud, making for the coin dropped by* **Mrs Needham**.

Harry My God.

Louisa (*gets the coin*) What do you want?

Harry Do you live under there?

Louisa Gives shelter from the wind, doesn't it?

Harry But how do you survive?

Louisa The wind blows particles of clever stuff all round me.

Harry I see. Are you alone?

Louisa Yes.

Harry What's it like?

Louisa It's sad.

Harry I'm sad too.

Louisa Don't come near me, I got a disease!

Harry Can I help?

Louisa No one can help. It just blows and blows and blows. And blows and blows and blows and blows and blows.

Harry I run a theatre. And I write the plays. They've just closed it down. That's why I'm sad.

Louisa My my. Dear dear. What a pity. – Look! (*She leaps across the mud.*) Lugworm! (*She scrabbles with her hands.*) Gone. Bugger! Not quick enough.

Harry I'm not allowed to work!

Louisa Very juicy, lugworms. I like a lugworm as a starter.

Harry What am I going to do? To hang on to my dignity?

Louisa I haven't got the faintest idea. I'm far too busy to go to the theatre. – Look! Out on the river! Oh look!

Harry Oh yes!

From the direction of the river, the sound of Handel's 'Water Music'. Coloured lights play on the mudbank as a boat glides slowly past. The sound of voices comes indistinctly from midstream.

I've never seen it before. And it is – despite everything, isn't it – amazingly beautiful . . .

Louisa Yes! Yes! – What is it?

Harry Why, it's the royal barge! And that one coming along behind is the barge for the musicians, do you see? That's an orchestra! Floating down the middle of the river! And look – there on the foredeck – that's the Queen!

Louisa The Queen?

Harry Yes, and there's bloody Walpole talking to her, kissing her hand! Oh, the bastard! You're an arsehole, Walpole! You're a shit!

Louisa Will you be quiet! That's the Queen, for goodness' sake! She doesn't want to hear that kind of language! (*She goes down on her knees in the mud.*) The Queen of England. All my life I've wanted to see the Queen, and now I have, it is complete. On my river! In front of my eyes! Your Majesty! Your Majesty!

Harry You're right. What point in yelling? Must find another way. Some system harder to control.

Louisa It's a royal wedding, is it? Oh I love a wedding! I love to see the happy bride! These people, they're so pretty, so clever! And the colours! And the music! And the flags!

Harry I'm thinking of writing a novel.

Louisa A what? What's one of them?

Harry Hard to explain. They're new.

*Blast of 'Water Music'. Slow fade on **Harry** and **Louisa**. The lights of the Royal Barge. The sounds of a party: laughter, conversation, glasses being smashed. Blackout.*

In the Ruins

In the Ruins was first broadcast by BBC Radio 3 on 3 June 1984 when the part of King George III was played by Nigel Stock. The play was directed by Richard Wortley, with music by Ilona Sekacz.

This revised edition, with the additional role of the Page, is scheduled to receive its first performance at the Bristol New Vic Theatre in 1989.

Characters:

King   *aged 77*

Page   *aged 12*

*The **King**'s apartment on the north terrace of Windsor Castle, circa 1817. A large, wood-panelled, wooden-floored room.* **George III** *is a very old man indeed. He has long white hair and beard, and wears a violet dressing gown.*

He sits at a harpsichord playing a slow section of Handel's 'Water Music Suite'. He plays at first correctly, but in a rather ponderous, child-like manner.

In the room are a decanter of water, glasses, many papers and scrolls, quill-pen and inkpot, and a naval-style flute.

*Soon the **King**'s playing starts to degenerate. Before long it is barely recognisable as Handel. It becomes demented, yet played with the utmost decorum. Suddenly he decides it is finished.*

King Aaah. Used to enjoy that when I was alive. Ah yes. Podgy old Herr Handel. A man of most prodigious – noise. He wrote that tune for my great-grandfather. No? Yes. Doubtless he's dead now, been dead for years. As indeed have I. Years and happy years before the flood Handel waddled round London with my great-grandpa but we're all three dead now and something died along with us too.

Dear old plinkety-plonkety Handel; at least he's buried; thank God, they have had the decency to stitch up his eyelids and inter him into the earth. Me, no. Me, no. Me, never. Oh, say a prayer for poor old George, a good and pious man who loved his God and some of his people and yes yes yes loved God and they forsake me. The inferior sort. They leave me . . . to continue. Hah! I here determine I shall live to be an hundred from sheer damned spite! – forsaken and forsook and damn it all abandoned dressed in my purple shroud. Ah. Ah. Ah. Ah. Mr Secretary make a fair copy of that Pronouncement and post it at the entrance to this cold castle, that the freezing-folk of Windsor may read. Now. Let the audience begin.

He claps his hands and greets an imaginary court.

Hullo, hullo. How do, good day. Come in, come in. (*Furiously.*) Come in! Ah yes. And you are the Ambassador for – where? What? What? No I've never been there. But was my playing good? or poor? or was it poor? Good? Bravo! You may rise. I did perceive it as good, within the narrow confines of my daily-blooded skull. I must frankly admit, sir, with no boasting, 'twas good.

For I will not boast. I will not brag. I do not pretend to any superior abilities. But I will give place to no one in meaning to preserve the freedom, happiness and glory of my dominions and all their inhabitants, though I am not an accomplished musician, and not one of those puking babies who crawl round the royal courts of Europe with their spindly hands out viz that Mozart I saw years and years and happy years ago before I passed away and didn't go to heaven. He was eight. The blubbing boy was eight years old and could play anything on sight. Bah! I loathed him. Eight! Unpardonable brilliance! Bah. Stretch the fabric of your imagination and picture my humble paltry self, fidgeting with embarrassment in the presence of Wolfgang Mozart, pooh and pooh again. But on no occasion do I perform Mozart's trivia when alone as I am most of the time or with my wife who does strum on the guitar with a most palatable mediocrity or indeed even with pleasant abstemious company like yourself, sir. I am glad now I recognise you as the Ambassador for – the what? That's a long way away. Report that I play Handel but never Mozart. They are both dead which is a point in their favour but I own I thought Handel died ever so much more graciously than that boastful boy and I hope if God wills it to do the same when my times comes which I heartily wish it would.

I thought I played my keyboard piece jolly well. No? Pretty fair? Not genius. Not Mozart- pozart. But fairly fair, between the ears, under the periwig, wouldn't you say? Hey? Hey? For sadly . . . for tragically . . . I cannot *see*, my estimable friends, to read the music. Or yet find the music. (*Laughs.*) Or yet look in the glass to see the sores where they put leeches to my temples. Or yet point at the harpsichord itself – which is not very old, it belonged to Queen Anne – if you turned me around and around and around and around. Doctors tried that oh yes long ago before the flood.

The Willises. Terrible men.

I'll tell you. The blackest of hearts. And to a man who is blind! Sightless. Blind. As a bat. As a bat. As a bat. As a bat. Fruit bat. Only luxury at the royal table. Favourite fruit of King: cherries. Favourite fruit of Queen: stewed pear. Favourite fruit of Prince of Darkness – (*Sudden change of tone.*) when normal we eat mutton chops and plum pudding. Yum yum. Won't get fat on that. Good English grub. And they say – the subjects, they say – the loving subjects – God preserve us from subjects – they calls us misers. Do! Yes they

do. Fruit bat. Bite you. Yah! – Sirs, madams, I crave forgiveness.
Thrift is a gift from God and it ill becomes the fiftieth King of
England to behave like a fruit bat. But I cannot see to bite the
music, though I play well and the blood drips down my chin,
middling well, don't I? Know it by heart, d'you see, luckily, learnt it
by heart, smart, hey? Water Music off by heart. Clever fellow, hey?
Hey? Clever old Nobs. Not mad at all. Smart in every particular.
Plays very very well . . .

I think.

I don't *hear* terribly clearly, d'you see. Not any more.

Makes playing music rather – but lucky I learnt those tunes, hey?
What? Lucky, what? What?

Yes.

He crashes his arms on to the keyboard.

Poor old fool gone mad thinks he's King of a time gone by.

Yes, King! *Avant le déluge*, at the very beginning of the reign, damn
near sixty year ago, with sight and hearing and in constant
communication with the Lord . . . issued a Proclamation. Yes. Did.

He blows a fanfare on an imaginary horn.

'A Proclamation for the Encouragement of Piety and Virtue, and
for the Preventing and Punishing of Vice, Profaneness and
Immorality. We do hereby declare our royal purpose and
resolution to discountenance and punish all manner of vice,
profaneness and immorality, particularly in such as are employed
near our royal person' – poor old beggar – 'And we do hereby
enjoin and prohibit all our loving subjects, of what degree or
quality soever, from playing on the Lord's day at dice, cards, or any
other game whatsoever; and we do hereby command and require
them decently and reverently to attend the Worship of God on
every Lord's day on pain of our highest displeasure and our Biting
out their Eyes.'

He snaps his teeth.

What? What? What? Vice? What? Send 'em home without any
supper. Oh, don't turn your face away, please madam, dear
madam, your pretty face, your perfect face with but a hint of blood
at the corners of the mouth, madam you have over-eaten again, no
please madam don't turn your face away, please madam the King is
talking to you! In the presence of a prince of the blood you will
stand next the wall and still your tongue! And God looked upon
the earth, and behold, it was corrupt!

(*Fatigued.*) The audience is over. You people may go.

He plays a few peculiar, wistful chords.

I wonder, does the Queen still live . . . ?

Wait! Don't go! I'm not finished.

I'm never finished.

Tell me, madam. Does the old croc live?

What? Say louder. Say louder. I cannot hear. Madam say louder!

It's hopeless and God said unto Noah the end of all flesh is come
before me for the earth is filled with violence through them and
behold I will destroy them with the earth. Charlotte . . . ? Alive . . . ?
Or croaked . . . ? I last saw the Queen for a quarter of an hour in
1812 I remember quite distinctly she smiled at me but with a tear in
her bulbous bloodshot piglike eye and she so dreadfully reduced
that her stays would wrap twice over I am damned I am damned I
am if I know what's the matter with the old girl who was always used
to eat her greens and I recall her then saying I had eyes like
blackcurrant jelly yes blackcurrant jelly pinpoints of hell in
shadowy sockets and would she kiss me? no the scoundrels
pinioned my arms when I tried to kiss my Queen but she did smile
at me – she did! – with her blotchy old face and this would be – let
me see – this would be – let me see – this would be – I'll reckon it
up now – this'd be about –

He bangs five times on the harpsichord case.

– five year ago. Well done. Five years. Good boy. Go to the top of
the family tree. Five happy years ago. Five vacuous, desolate years.

Since last I saw Charlotte my wife. And even then I was blind from my ages of crying and could but just feel the tremble of her little little wrinkled hand in my little little wrinkled hand only for a moment as we sat quiet and remembered . . .

And then of course I began talking again blasted fool. And she wept. (*Laughs gently.*) Crocodile tears. For with all the rest the Queen thinks the King's lost his head when in point of irredeemable fact he's the only monarch in Europe with a head left to stand his blasted crown upon, isn't he? (*He cries.*) Isn't he?

Never never never on any account leave me alone with the mad-doctors again I beg you Charlotte my dear love never never never never.

They tie me to my coronation chair. (*He laughs.*)

It is not funny! My mind is ulcered by the treatment that it meets from all around. They tie me down they tie me up I bite me tongue. They leech my head. They blister me feet with squashed beetles and mustard immerse me in boiling blood. I cut my face. They snatch my razor. They take my mirror. Lest I lick the blackcurrant jelly d'you see Lord Malmesbury. But I am blind I remind them I am blind I scream! – but these scoundrels in the mad-business are so jolly ignorant of anything at all, even gardening's a thing they know naught of, even I know a bit about veg, blockheads, the King is blind I say and nearly nearly deaf. So the page tilts my chair slightly at night to signify time for beddie-bye but no sweet dream or woolly blanket because first they do drag me through hideous hot baths ho! horrid hot waters and they manage me with great violence and want of due respect and then they strap me in my cot where I may not presume to sleep lest the waters creep by me in the night-time and I drown and all the affairs of state get sopping wet . . .

Ahem. The cause to which they all agree to ascribe the unfortunate calamity that is me is the force of a humour which was beginning to show itself in my legs some thirty odd years past when, so they say, my 'imprudence' and I hesitate to suggest the nature of this my 'imprudence' drove it from thence into my bowels which are an item I have long had cause to complain of as for example the streams of purplish water issuing therefrom and now d'you follow the medicines they were obliged to use for the preservation of my royal life viz the camphor the calomel the quinine the digitalis the tartarised antimony and so forth have repelled this malignant humour up upon the royal brainbox at which juncture – can I speak to you man to man my Lord? – the Willises and Sir George Baker who's waiting outside are strongly inclined to think the disorder permanent. This is despite the frequent application of the baths and the bloodings to divert these morbid humours from my anointed brow. Permanent. Hah!

(*Calls.*) Sir George Baker come in here at once! Stand still stop fumbling and say hullo to Lord Malmesbury. *He* is my friend. Ah. Ah. Hand me that paper. (*He finds a paper.*) 'His Majesty suffers an entire alienation of mind. Opinion of the Five Physicians.' Bah! Pooh! What cod is this? Sir Doctor George did you write this report? It is feeble, sir, feeble. My mind has never functioned better than it does this day. Were it not for the disabling fact that I am deceased, who can say what further glory might be Britain's?

D'you see you are I fear, or rather rejoice, quite mistaken in your diagnosis of my condition Sir George. It's only nervousness. I have always been a nervous sort as you know. Really you're nothing but an old hen. We shall deck you out in feathers. (*Laughs.*) Cackle cackle. Come along. Cackle.

He impersonates a hen.

Come along, now, cackle with the King! Cack cack cack and (*Checks himself.*) Hold. Hold! I am calm. But I am nervous. I am not ill, but I am nervous. If you would know what is the matter with me, I am nervous. Sir George you have said the shade by which soundness of mind is to be distinguished from some degree of insanity is often faint, and in many cases hardly perceptible. Now there is an enormous burden of truth in that and it is an exceptionally fortunate thing for the British Empire and Dominions that it is only my slight attacks of nerves that you have mistaken for lunacy in the space between my ears and it's a confusion that could happen to anyone even dimwit physicians now if you would have the good grace to send for my naval uniform and have them unlock the door –

He goes to a bolted door and rattles it violently.

– we'll go a walk in Windsor without any attendants, shall we? You

could not possibly hope to meet a more rational monarch than
George the Third in the whole of history, man. Pray do not forget
you are merely a Knight of the Bedchamber and entirely
dependent on me for advancement.

As I say it is but a minor attack of nerves similar to that which struck
me down in 1765 and again in 1788 and again in 1801 and again in
1804 – look I recall the dates well – and the reason I have by this last
onslaught been mildly incapacitated for six and a half years is
entirely due to there being a terrible lot to be nervous about. I own
I incline too much to our John Bull, and am apt to despise what I
am not accustomed to, and with this despising comes a sort of fear.
I am utterly blind and almost deaf and the balance of my mind has
proved inaccurate – but yet I am Your Majesty and I will not be held
prisoner in my own castle in this obscene fashion. I have taken a
solemn determination that unless I am this day allowed to go over
to the house where the Queen and my family are, no earthly
consideration shall induce me to sign my name to any paper or to
do one act of government whatever! Then let's see how the nation
gets along! What? What? What? . . . Any further talk of a Regency,
Sir traitor George, sir, and I shall consign you to a certain inferno
of my acquaintance.

Oh my dear Lord Bute of Long Ago, come forward, my loved one,
you will put in a good word for me I feel certain. I do talk perfectly
coherent as you see. I am now much weaker than I was, yes, yes, but
as an example of my clearheadedness I have prayed to God all
night that I might die, or that he would spare my reason. And as
you see both of these things have gloriously come to pass. I am
swimming for the Lord in the waters of night. I am trying to talk as
slowly as possible for one with a devil of a lot going back and forth
around the skull. Stay with me and hold my hand a moment for I
cannot stop shaking and my pulse gallops like the winner at
Newmarket. Oh, I have the most profound consciousness of terror,
my dear, dear love, for I cannot find the Queen of my Heart and I
shan't be allowed on the Ark without her. My footsies are swollen
and I've a lingering pain in the gut. In the translation of this
pestilential flying disorder from one part to another, the horrid
thing appears to have become locally fixed on the brain which is
the most appalling tragedy for a fellow who was used to take clocks
and chronometers apart and what is more put them back together
again with the aid of only three of four servants. I insist upon
walking on the Terrace on occasion, that members of the public

might know without question I am still at work despite having died. But it is so hard dearest Bute to explain to folk what it is like internally to be this nervous when one is regularly put bawling in the straight-waistcoat by those vile men and left trussed like a breast of lamb and this is why I'm telling you that the King is *not* alienated in the head and *not* dangerous and *not* hungry for his bone and doesn't require *any more* hot baths thank you for I will not throw my Kingdom into confusion by pretending to be alive when I ain't and this is why you'd better let me out on the terrace where I can keep a blind eye on my empire for I've the flying gout they say it flew from my paws to my silly old head – *and* I've to think of my crocodile wife with gargantuan mouth and my lovely darling daughters who read to me in my darkness and hold my jelly hand and this is why I've been saved from the slavering jaws of death with the aid of Master Noah and his splendid rowing boat and this is why I am perfectly fit for the office of King except alas that my water gushes the colour of port wine and stains my breeches and this is why they wrap me legs in flannel which I don't think seemly for the most magnificent majesty walking on the oceans but please big sirs and bloated madams don't you know I am not ill but I am nervous so nervous I cannot keep still no I cannot keep static still incontinents to conquer and my men are on the job second sons of adventure all covered in gore but God it's a nerve-wracking business this ruling the world and I own I am prone to jump at the sound of my own voice wohah! for I don't . . . d'you see I don't hear it very often and when I do it is always talking such bosh always have the suspicion I am talking talking talking talking far too speedily Malmesbury and far too much and rattling away and heaven knows what and I know this and I know that and I can hear it I can hear it I can hear it now – my God what say I in my delirium! respecting this or that or Lady Pembroke's smelly fanny way way down in the hairy valley of perfect peace – I can hear it again! what torture! what pain! to hear what is said by means of words this fellow is *mad* and shouldn't be followed with the royal diadem of purple piss upon his head the sceptre in his skinny hand 'Rex Insanit' say the Seven Physicians! Damn I can still touch! Damn I can still smell! Lord it is too much take me and drown me in rivers of blood where we win all the battles and never lose colonies or ever outlive our allotted span or glug! or silence! or glug! or silence! silence in the vale of tears!

The **King** *raves. The heavy bolts on the outside of the door are drawn back and a* **Page** *enters. He is an angelic-looking boy of about 12, in livery. He runs to the* **King** *and forces a large handkerchief into his mouth. Then he* *steps back. The **King** thrashes around a little more but then subsides. Pause. The **Page** steps forward and removes the gag from the **King**'s mouth. He helps the **King** up and steers him to his harpsichord stool. The **King** sits and plays a phrase rather badly. He sings in a hoarse, cracked voice (Recitative No. 17 from Handel's 'Messiah'):*

'Then the eyes of the blind shall be opened, and the ears of the deaf unstoppéd: then shall the lame man leap as an hart, and the tongue of the dumb shall sing.'

*He finishes playing. The **Page** pours a large glass of water and hands it to him. The **King** drinks it fast and scrabbles around for a piece of paper.*

Here comes the latest bulletin. 'Opinion of the Eleven Physicians: The King is dead long live the King.' Oh – jolly good. That's more like it. I am coming, Master Noah, pipe me aboard, up the gangplank, two by two. Ah. Ah. Excellent. Excellent. But you have want of a fruit bat I notice. 'Of fowls after their kind, and of cattle after their kind, of every creeping thing of the earth after his kind,' sayeth the Holy Book. That includes bats. Have you a cabin for my Charlotte and I, Noah? With a porthole that faces north? We don't like the sun. For, sir, a most dreadful flooding of purple water has submerged London city of the gallows and everything that is in the earth has died. And I would be happy on the Ark where on the land I sorrowed.

Page. Give me a pen.

*The **Page** gives him a quill-pen and ink. The **King** scratches furiously.*

Now go away – I've a composition to do.

*The **Page** goes to a corner of the room, where he finds some of the inner workings of a large clock, which he begins to re-assemble.*

'Reflections on the Present State of the Navy and the Reasons why the Fleet is not in Greater Forwardness than it is.'

He suddenly stops writing.

Why? Why? Why me? Why do these imbecilic chores always fall to me? Because I am Rex Insanit I suppose. 'His Majesty is multifarious in his questions, but thank God he answers them all himself.' Thus Samuel Johnson, damned scoundrel. Calls himself a doctor couldn't bleed the cholic off a cow. Come come Johnson, speak up. By what authority words in the dictionary may I consider my naked corpse better than that of some miserable petty . . . baronet, say? (*Laughs.*) I jest of course. Get out of my library, Johnson. Oh, and collect up those documents, in case they get wet.

He throws bundles of official papers everywhere, laughing. The **Page** *just watches as they flutter down around his head.*

What? What? Wet? Go sink in the salty sea three times but only come up twice. If my work on the Navy's got wet . . .! Oh I despair! This is the wickedest age that ever was seen. An honest man must wish himself out of it. Yes. Yes. Yes. Yes. I begin to be heartily sick of the things I daily see – for ingratitude, avarice and ambition are the principles men act by nowadays, nothing whatever to do with our what? our what? our God-given time-honoured national order of magnitude which holds that I and I alone am fit to rule, that Lord Bute is to sit beside me and hold my jelly, that Parliament's to do what it's told, that a Duke comes first before a Marquis, that there is an extremely sensible distinction to be made between an Earl and a Viscount, and damn it all a mighty profitable reward to be had from making it! All of which is prior to even proposing for consideration the middling sort, the stock-jobbers, moneylenders, seekers of improvement and oh the mob. Peers and commoners alike, may I remind you sirs that a King does not solicit advice, he gives orders! I will have no innovation in my time despite the drivel and dross of those whatyoumecallem hell-begotten Jacobines across the foaming sea . . . signing Declarations of this, that and the other . . . Independence . . . Rights of stupid Man . . . bah! look what's befallen them savages now . . . away across the sea . . . cruel wretches who have possessed themselves of power God gouge their eyes . . . over there . . . across the slimy sea . . .

Pause. Then a memory which delights him.

I saw a bridge.

I saw an iron bridge!

Marvellous thing in every particular, my dearest Lady Pembroke. Bridge made of iron. Aye! My lady you possess everything a hungry bat could want beneath the foldings of your silks and velvets. Oh me oh my. And let me tell you of my manufactures, the length and breadth of the land! Such progress! Great strides leaps bounds and forward march! Clever men, very clever men, bless my soul, monstrously clever men whom we admire without limit. The coming men. The new order. The things they make for me! Beautiful machines! Pretty pretty! Clockses oh watches oh barometers hygrometers chronometers microscopes telescopes . . . Mr Herschel built me a giant telescope for purposes of looking at Uranus, my Lady. My new planet. And with my telescope I can see Hanover. Look! Dry land, Noah! I can see Germany! For the first time ever by God! Here's I plodding along ploughboy-fashion at the sharp end of the Hanoverian dynasty and I'm the only beggar never to have seen the place! Damn me! I can see Hanover. But not America. Oh blast. Was hoping to avoid (*Change.*) now a hygrometer d'you see is a useful device bless me yes, applicable to the management of the moisture and temperature of the hot and green houses of our botanical establishment at Kew for I grow turnips d'you see. Exotic plants. Slimy green fingers of the King. What? Yes. King George Three. Lives in England, likes it. Ordinary man. Pleasant chap. Farmer George. With his sheep corn spuds turnips. Much loved. Talks to the people. And at Worcester, my Lady, we gave three cheers for the new bridge built of iron and for three good fellows all called George for a hundred years for a new era wrought of iron and a million machines for spinning and weaving and ploughing and seeding and coal and canals and banging and blasting and bridges and boats and buying and selling and sailing the seas!

He's over-excited. The **Page** *mops his brow.*

. . . Ever hear of a noisy item called a Steam Engine? Hey?

I've one. I've many. Oh-ho yes, two chaps called Boulton and Watt build 'em. Not here, no. Not in Windsor or London or Kew, spoil the view. Away to the north in the wastelands of my Kingdom. I don't like the barren ugly scarcely populated northern shires, my Lady, I prefer Windsor Forest which is immeasurably more perfect than anywhere else d'you see, and also much nearer to hand. I have no taste for what are called the fine wild beauties of nature, I do not like mountains and other such romantic scenes, of which I sometimes hear much. Never seen 'em, of course. Never been norther of Worcester or souther of Weymouth. What's the point?

What my Lady?

(*Furious.*) I know there are insurrections and tumults in every far-flung corner of the farmyard! This King still has his head stuck on, madam, and still his black eyes see – there is no government, no law! What's that my little squirrel? Aye I do know why! For when religion and public spirit are quite absorbed by vice and dissipation, this sort of havoc is the natural consequence. Even, 'twould seem, at court. For, if we squint through our cataract of tears, do we perceive you squatting on your fat seditious hams? We do! I am standing on my two hind legs why are not you? Get up! Have I not said I will have no republics in *my* pigsty? And are the rest of you all with this rutting Pembroke bitch who's in disgrace? Get up I say! Here, Mr Secretary, I'll make my mark on her death warrant. We will restore some dignity to the method of proceeding with these audiences. Who said they could sit? Here we are. (*Scratches with pen.*) 'George' . . . jolly good . . . and 'R' . . . damn my watery joints . . . and 'R' . . . there! What? Pretty well for a man who is mad. Hang the whore tomorrow.

The **Page** *slams down the lid of the harpsichord with a bang.*

. . . I love my subjects but why do they plague me so?

I know what it is. What? I know what it is. What? Do I? Yes. It's because I lost America. That's the ticket. It's because I lost America that's what it is. Had the blasted thing a second ago and now where is it? Where? Where is it? Where's Amerikey? Over the sea? Devil take the place. Not a simple task, I will allow, to lose something as apparently substantial as half a continent, but I your King have done it. Abject failure. Pleasant chap but consigned to the small print. Poor old Nobs, the loving subjects despise me for losing America. Bad for trade. Slaves in particular. And left us with nowhere to dump our convicts. Hah! Discovered Australia, didn't we? Ever resourceful. Captain Cook. Good fellow I've shook his Yorkshire hand. Botany Bay. Long way. But we had of course worked out arithmetically that there must be a huge southern land-mass to counterbalance Europe, or God's great world would have toppled over years ago. We are ever mindful of the contribution of science to our illustrious reign.

(*Sadly.*) But I that am born a gentleman shall never rest me head on me last pillow in peace as long as I remember the loss of my

American colonies. For this squander of a cornered market, I beg forgiveness, Oh my Lord, oh my people.

He prays a little.

I've never been over the sea. I've been *in* the sea. Go bathing in the briny good for the pores. When I disappear beneath the waves the band plays the national anthem which do demonstrate how popular I be. At Portsmouth. Or Weymouth. Or Bournemouth. Or Plymouth. May I say, one cannot move in this country without meeting a myriad *mouths*, there's a snapping of teeth a slapping of lips there's a grasping snatching idle pauper person concealed in every fold of the hills and crying out for bread! bread! when we are desperately trying to sleep . . . there is hunger in the land, I know, but I am frugal, it is not my fault . . . I simply cannot sleep curse it . . . They surround my carriage, d'you see, wantonly breaking the windows with musket shot and pebbles and crying out for food, but the critical thing sirs and madams is that we *do not show fear* no matter how sticky it be in your britches. At the last counting I can recall precisely two verifiable attempts on my royal life, not including the deeds of doctors specially engaged in the department of insanity, nor the time I was attacked as I drove to the state opening of Parliament, let me see let me figure say five or six years after the fall of the Bonbons in Paris. On that occasion the mob, no doubt aggravated by all that French fol-de-rol and spurred on by bloody Voltaire and double-bloody Thomas Paine I fully expect, crushed against the gilded carriage yelling 'Peace and bread! No war with the French Republic!' Bah. 'No war! No King! Down with George!' This is precisely what I have this last half hour been attempting to warn you about, gentlemen of the House, from the vantage of my loftier position. I appeal to your nicer instincts. Think! King Mob on the loose . . . stocks and shares in decline . . . the Crown in peril. I appeal to you! What we are now placing under investigation, viz, the developments in France with respect to monarchs – head and shoulders, continued union of – is as far removed from the peace and serenity of our good old English ways as are all we decent law-abiding citizens from the dirt and heat and smells of damned Australia! God perserve us the scruffiest urchin of the street may now be heard belching the foul garlic-breath of republicanism and God bless us demanding a vote in the constitution of this House! Undoubtedly, if that sort of ballyhoo holds good it is diametrically opposite to what I have known all my life. The Crown rests.

He sits, pleased with himself. The **Page** *pours him some more water which he gulps down. The* **Page** *pours him the rest, then exits with the empty jug.*

Water is held to be unhealthy in these parts but the King drinks gallons of the stuff and pray remark the excellent condition of his coat. Spa water for preference, barley water for a special occasion, and no need for recourse to the rhubarb pills.

Where was I? Indeed where am I? Oh.

Once upon a time a domestic called Margaret Nicholson sought with the aid of a kitchen knife to slice us into cutlets on the very steps of our palace at St. James's. The heaving cheering crowd, good English peasants all, some having walked for days to see us in our splendour, made to rip her limbs from their sockets exactly as one pulls the wings off a chicken. No! we cry. Hold! The poor creature is inevitably mad. Do not hurt her! The poor creature is mad! Who but a simpleton would have motive to murder *me*?

The girl was spared and led to Bedlam it is my happy duty to report.

As for the other fellow's cowardly attack, in the year of 1800, well, bless me, his brain had been damaged by sabre-wounds in my son the Duke of York's campaign against Bonaparte. Not only was this witless assassin not in his right mind but alas and alack his mind had been perfunctorily divided into segments like an orange and knowing which portion to reside his thoughts in would have put to the test many a better thinker than he. The royal party was at Drury Lane theatre where we often went when I was alive to see a nice genteel sort of comedies with no profanity and Charlotte the Queen held my little pink blancmange. I put my opera-glass to my still-seeing eye and look about the house for pretty young squirrels as is my wont when on an instant boom! boom! two shots whip past my still-hearing ear and as I later learn one kills the lion and the unicorn is mortally splintered. The Queen, dear heart, is preoccupied with feeding sweetmeats to her lapdogs and fails to note the piercing choral shriek of our assembled Princesses. I stand perfectly still. I look about regally as before. Subsequently I am complimented on my composure I will have you know. Hah! Composure! I thought it was part of the play . . .

He laughs sourly at the memory.

Hmm. I am sensible of having been much out of order, Sir George,
but I am at present lucid d'you notice. When I am composed I talk
sense and take a paternal interest in the running of things, but
when nervous I am prone to babble and speaking in tongues. For
so long as I am agitated by nobody in this chill castle, I am perfectly
easy to get along with. I trust you will mark my words, Baker, and
(*Whispers.*) defend me from mine enemies. My singular enemy is
Doctor blasted Willis God rot his danglies. This is a man gave up
the Church, an honourable profession, for medicine, one I heartily
despise. The weasel defends this calumny with the probably
blasphemous claim that Our Saviour himself went about healing
the sick. Well I have had a word or two with the Archbishop on this
exceeding nice point of theology, Sir Knight of the Bedpan, and
the upshot is yes, yes, yes, we concede he *did*, but he did not get
seven hundred a year for it, did he! But the hateful Willises father
and son will not accept the superiority of my logic, and they stitch
me in the restraining-chair for the making of the slightest sound
and if I am bad they bind me to my coronation oath! Oh my dear
dead Amelia, why won't you save your father? These scoundrels
have the blackest hearts in the history of colour. I hate all
physicians. But most I hate the Willises. Send 'em home without
any grub.

He cries a little. The **Page** *re-enters with fresh water. He sees the* **King** *crying
and goes to comfort him. He holds the* **King***'s hand tenderly.*

Oh, thank you. I feel quite tired now. I once had a hankering for a
frisky Irish filly who thought me a bore but the Privy Council settled
me unseen on a German, my beloved Charlotte of the sharp
snapping teeth, and I was obliged to contract quick as the market
in eligible, royal, protestant cunts was at that juncture quite
impoverished. But since my Charlotte came to England I have
loved her as a leech loves blood. Aah, yes. But now the subjects say I
kept my young wife a virtual prisoner when first she came to this
gruesome peasant land. Well, um, I did, yes. I wished to shield my
blushing croc from the poisons and oh the corruptions of the age. I
have already talked I think of the wholesale vice and dissipation
here and the moves that were going forward on our part against it. I
must declare our every effort a pitiful failure. Every single decree
unheeded. Every act unheard. Every proclamation announced to
an empty market square. The subjects blind and deaf to my will and
as sinful as ever they were, possibly more so since the advent of this
Freethinking la-de-da. Drat! One can try devilish hard to be good,
and still be held a sinner.

And there is another reason why my Queen was rarely seen abroad in your poxed and reeking London society. Before she was forty years of age she had at my behoof presented you ungrateful dogs with fifteen little Princes and Princesses. Fifteen! I know them all by name. Even the bloody boys. – But my lovely darling daughters have stayed with me in my infirmity and never married no husband good enough and though rather old now they are terribly terribly content and would simply not dream of going away – not that I'd allow it of course I've enough troubles as I've made quite clear. Amelia is my favourite because she's dead and will hold my hand in heaven.

I was a good father. I mean, I was good at fathering. Unless you are good at *something*, you cannot be of utility to your country, nor credit to your family. I am a family man living the clean life of a country squire with my sheep and my turnips and enjoying my nuptial rights almost without limit. Aaah yes. (*Yawns.*) That's surely no bad thing for a King, to live a simple life, and take simple pleasures . . . oh . . . I strive to recall the tremor in my loins when she first (*Change.*) I take great joy in my patriotic duty and so I believe does my endearingly rigid partner, and I offer as proof that between us we have produced not only a lawful heir to the throne damn his profligate eyes but also a full team of quite legitimate reserves. I do sometimes wonder whether I be at all different in these respects, and in my method of going about it, from any malodorous farmboy up a milkmaid in the hay but the answer is a foregone conclusion so I don't waste my clockwork upon it. Bless my soul I am getting tired. Been King for nearly sixty year. And with all my heart I wish my wife would unbolt that door and come and kiss me now on my watery eyes . . . for how else will I know she is alive?

Charlotte . . .?

Dear friends, I must sleep as I have great want of that refreshment. This levee is adjourned. (*Prays.*) Almightly God and Admiral Noah, settled in the joys of death I shut my eyes, amen.

Behold the unplumbed sea of dreams.

His eyes wide open, staring.

Drat. Wide awake. Ships of the line at Portsmouth, that usually helps. An hundred guns: HMS Victory, HMS Britannia, HMS Royal Sovereign. Ninety-eight guns: HMS Neptune, HMS Temeraire, HMS Dreadnought, HMS Prince. Seventy-four guns: HMS Leviathan, HMS Conqueror, HMS Ajax, HMS Orion, HMS Minotaur, HMS Swiftsure, HMS Mars, HMS Colossus, HMS Bellerophon, HMS Revenge, HMS . . . Belleisle . . . HMS . . . and all the rest . . . sail on to glory at Trafalgar . . . aar . . .

*With a sigh, he falls asleep. The **Page** waits for a moment and then disengages himself from the **King**. The **King** breathes peacefully. He snores once, twice. The **Page** exits, bolting the door behind him. As soon as he is gone the **King** wakes in a fury and leaps around the room.*

GNNNNNNAAAAAAAAAARGH! Ireland! Bad dream! Bloody dream! Ireland!

Blast and smite and roast the papists for intruding on my private dreams! I am a tolerant man but these pisspot Catholics go too damn far!

Ireland, pah! Not another mention of the bog-ridden place! Am I fully understood? . . . Ssssh. It's somewhere we've never heard of, children, a wretched dark land full of witches and leper-corns and wafer-munching monsignors. But we have a lovely big army and a lovely big navy and we shall bring light and contentment to those desert shores. Now hush! boys and girls, not a word more. I wave my arms and away it goes – voila!

He plays a merry tune to take his mind off it.

Ah me. Dreams. I once, my dear Bute, dreamt I was making a speech at the Lord Mayor's banquet, and when I woke up I found I was. Ho ho ho ho ho ho ho. Broke bread that day with a Quaker fellow name of Barclay, David Barclay. The King likes Quakers simple people no ostentation. Brother Barclay's doing pretty well started up a bank I do believe. I like a man with the sniff of success about him but not flaunting it under one's nose like the dull Mozart of ancient memory and we have I am told created the perfect climate for bankers, what with the investments in India and the price of blacks and so forth. Yes yes. You mark my words.

Yes. But I must beg pardon for I don't understand money. I try but I don't understand. Look here for an example. I sell my sheep at

Smithfield Market sheep fed on turnips I understand *that* I know
my Rural Economy madam, turnip-fed sheeps give dung and dung
giveth forth turnips hip! hip! huzza! God's mighty circulations, and
my sheep sell at fourpence ha'penny a pound in Smithfield Market,
all to the good so far, but now d'you see the cooks at the Queen's
House – Buckingham House where my Lady keeps her pet
elephants – say they are paying a shilling for mutton. We are
seriously confused. The butcher fellow at the Queen's House is a
slippery fish with a rollmop tongue so I sent for him I was nervous
so I sent for him hey butcher! stand up man you have legs not fins
and butcher! explain! I sell my turnip-fed sheep to your man at
market for fourpence ha'penny, and what do you sell 'em back to
the Queen's kitchen for? A shilling! Damn me damn you and damn
the animals, a shilling a pound for the exact same sheep only
deader and cut into chops! Bless us and save us! That's a
whatyoumecallit of sevenpence-ha'penny! Now what pray is the
ultimate fate of those extraneous monies? Master butcher, will you
please account! Tell me what I want to know and I'll give you a glass
of barley water. There is something going forward here that we
cannot precisely put our finger on. But as I have said I don't follow
money matters too dogmatically. I've no spare cash for I've spent
all me money on bribes. Are you at all aware that the vote of a
prominent landowner or East Indiaman may cost as much as a
brand-new barometric clock? And by Jesus he may not even be
titled nowadays never mind ticking or chiming or pointing to
Squalls! Is it any wonder I am nervous, pretty madam? Damn my
boots, in a country where we permit a full quarter million men to
vote you'd expect a handful to poll freely in my favour! Well, well,
well, my ministers assure me I need not worry, as no up-to-date
government would be so incompetent as to lose an election. But yet
it is *my* pockets being dipped and delved into, and *tradesmens'*
pockets being lined! What? Yes! What? Preposterous. And now this
brine-soaked butcher has told me a lie. A white lie, he says, but I
hate a white lie. If you will tell me a lie, then let it be a black lie.
Black is the shade I am seasoned to. Black is the sheep for me.

Oh me flock have all gone astray, all run off to market at a
knockdown price and because I am me I can't haggle. Come back!
Back!

He whistles like a shepherd. The **Page** *enters and watches him.*

Here boy! Back into the fold! Here my bonny lass! Bah. Hey!

Farmer George is speaking! You listen to your squire! . . . Oh, what
point is there my sitting on the five-bar gate and giving you
bumpkins advice? You will not act upon it. Yet I that am born for
the happiness or misery of a great nation, a tower of babel, a silly
old fool with a strong constitution, am given to speak the remains
of my mind . . . oh, I'm in the grip of an evil humour but I have no
heart to laugh.

He plays a few very sad chords.

Little little lambs, I do feel the warmest gratitude for the support
and anxiety shown by the nation at large during my recent tedious
illness and I am sorry that a prompting was required. Do but not
scamper off to market without me, and there would be no need for
this ceaseless slaughter of the innocents, would there, Master
butcher? For the Holy Scripture tells you, Fear God, Honour the
King. And latterly a saddening high proportion of our once-loyal
subjects are instead lending their allegiance to this hot devil's
breath Electricity. I smell a treason . . . Ah, but we tire of talking of
it. Matters of science will often derange simple country folk. Hey,
ho, diddley-ay-day. Not long past we did get ourselves into a fearful
stew over the trivial question of oh lightning conductors – ends of,
pointed or blunt more effective. Silly little fat boy Franklin. Flies
kites. In storm and rain a stormbrain. Perfectly good hunting
weather, too.

He bays like a hound and toots an imaginary hunting horn. The **Page** *joins
in the game. He climbs on the* **King***'s back and they gallop happily round the
room, the* **Page** *whipping the* **King***'s flanks.*

Page Giddy-up! Giddy-up!

But soon the pleasure of the game subsides for the **King.**

King Now this double-damned Benjamin Franklin took himself
over to the hell-begotten French and by Jesus got 'em in the
American war against us. Natural enemies of course on a par with
the Willises when it comes to trickery. We would not have lost
otherwise, for we meant well to the Americans, just to punish them
with a few bloody noses and then shake hands for the mutual
happiness of our two countries. Sporting gesture. Very English.
Then along from the jaws of death belches modern man Franklin,
evil republican beggar, and damn me is heard to express the hope

that I might forego the use of lightning conductors altogether and thus bring down the thunder of heaven upon my poor decrepit head! Bless my soul and thank God the sword is my shepherd! And thank God for the Iron Duke of Wellington, and thank God for lowness and thank God for highness! For where would I be if all men were peers?

He sings in a cracked voice from the 'Hallelujah Chorus':

'Hallelujah! Hallelujah! And it shall rain for ever and ever! And it shall rain –'

He suddenly stops, puzzled.

Now here's me predicament, butcher: Franklin insists on pointed ends and hang me the Royal blasted Society has the gall to say he's right. I back blunted ends, d'you see, on a whim – which turns out to be wrong. But it is it not well known the King can do no wrong? So. What? Why? Which? My mind is in turmoil and my piss the colour of blood, (*Softly.*) for the awful dawning between the royal ears is that all these spinning mules and rolling locomotives and suchlike industrial whatdoyoucallems do more or less presage a turnabout in the wondrous God-given pattern of English life and I am agin turnabouts as I have repeatedly said. I have the fullest confidence in Divine Providence of course but can our smoking pulsating new cities be ruled by the village idiot? Oh 'tis most perplexing. The very thing that makes us great I fear brings on our ending. No! Surely! Tell me, Mr Ambassador, sir, what does the future hold? Oh I don't know if I can endure it!

He cries in bewilderment. The **Page** *is bored.*

Well will you look at this French Turnabout for an example? Bonaparte and the hounds of hell? The swish of the murderous guillotine? – which is a triumph of precision engineering and invented in Halifax, Yorkshire. I will not pretend I was not at first heartened, to see peacock Louis Bonbon a-sinking in the mire – but God preserve us to chop him up like firewood! 'Tis inhuman! and quite against the law! Yet we should not be surprised at anything these trouserless savages might do. All Europe is in flames! . . . except, um, Windsor. Hmm. But there is at large in our land a species of thing called a Reforming Society if you ever heard so much codswallop. Legacy of that devil Wilkes. Blasted

commoner spews sedition! – and every time my men expel him
from Parliament, the double-damned voters elect him back in
again. I am afraid I have been forced to declare the loser the
winner and sling Wilkes in the Tower. Cost an absolute mint! And
now a thing called a Society for Constitutional Information so help
me God! The Constitutional Information is, that *I am here*! Decked
out in me purple splendour! Now go home and be quiet.

The **Page** *has found the flute. He plays a few tentative notes on it. They
permeate the* **King***'s consciousness; he listens intently. The Page plays a
sea-shanty. The* **King** *tried to dance a hornpipe, which exhausts him very
quickly.*

Nelson.

Where's Nelson.

Where's half-pint? Is he among ye? I'll tell you something. He's
dead too. Lord Nelson. One gets along best with corpses. I'll tell
you something else. Died at Battle of Trafalgar. Great hero. Dying
wish: to be buried in English soil. Good fellow. Problem: length of
voyage, Trafalgar to here, three months. Now in three months a
devil of a lot of decay can occur to a chap who's deceased. Solution,
courtesy brain of ship's doctor: embalm him in a cask of rum. Jolly
good. Duly carried out. Small chap, perfect fit. Subsequent
dreadful realisation on part of officers in wardroom: rum is not nor
never shall be a gentleman's drink. Whip him out. Duly done. Put
him a cask of *brandy*. Same effect overall, and without any lowering
of fit and proper standards. Officers go three months without a
drink but Nelson arrives home to our ultimate accolade I shake his
pickled hand and give him a hero's funeral. All true.

Ah there you are. Lord Nelson of the Nile. You did not mind our
creating you a peer of 'the Nile', did you, my short friend? Only we
know you have unfortunately no estate, d'you see, and although we
aren't a skinflint, setting you up with a few hundred choice acres in
Dorset was more than the royal budget would permit . . . But you
don't object? Splendid! The Nile is yours, then! Plant whatever you
like! Spuds are a damn good bet. Now come here kneel down let
me give you your next command.

We go to a hideous noisy war. – Have you ever stopped to consider,
Admiral, how if our manufacturing fellows had not mastered the

casting of iron frames, no one could have invented the pianoforte
and the world would have been spared the horrors of Beethoven?
However, without our iron foundries we should not have been able
to build such splendid big cannon, should we? Hmm . . . which to
choose . . . good music, or total domination of the map? – Ahem.
This is quite simply a war for the preservation of society. We must
vanquish the republican dragon and restore the natural order.
On account of being blind and deaf I shall deal with the domestic
end of things, yes yes yes, that is traditional, and till driven to the
wall I certainly will do what I can to save the Empire from this
Corsican adventurer – and if I do not succeed, I will at least have
the self-approbation of having done my duty. A thing my Lord
Nelson I believe you are acquainted with. As to yourself, I will never
doubt that, whenever it shall please the Almighty to permit an
English fleet fairly to engage any other, a most comfortable issue
will arise. Ah indeed. For I am a man of the sea. The sea is in my
blood. Whereas, Admiral, your blood is in my sea. Hmm. Lowly
chap, no sense of protocol.

Yes the ocean's a perilous place. I'm the old captain so I'll stay at
home. You Jack Tar defend me. For I've stood on the sea wall at
Portsmouth and watched the chain be hung across the harbour
mouth to keep at bay the Frenchies, and the waves roll in hard and
black the colour of iron, and the huge chain's of iron, and the sky's
an industrial grey, and a molten lead rain blanks out the Island,
and forty days and forty nights, and the chain and the sea and the
sky and the rain and it's too vast and too wet for me and I'm back in
me greenhouse at Kew where I've a few experiments going off. His
botanic Majesty. Head down here look there's two turnips rutting
in a bucket of manure – marvellous sight in every particular – and
very quiet too. I hope you can run the railway of my thought, dear
old Bute, for in fact I love the deep sea dearly. I go boating at
Weymouth, row the wife and the little ones in ten-oar cutters. Go
swimming in the deep blue blood. At Weymouth they have cut my
picture in their chalky hill. Hooray! I like my subjects. But why will
they never settle? Give thanks to God they're British and form up in
order of precedence? But no. But no. I've seen such confusion and
distraction in this too much divided land. I've seen the twitching
drooling gob guzzle guzzle gobble gobble coast to coast and
grinning like a valet when the Queen breaks wind, ever eating,
loving subjects, ever stuffing, devouring with their champing
chomping teeth, boiled beef roast beef roast pike pig's face pork's
neck sheep's heart gooseberry sauce lamb chop yum yum hams and

mint and fishies veal and onion meat and eat tart jelly and syllabub pears plums cream and butter eat and eat and eat your meat fat English, look at 'em, staggering around with a bellyful of puke. Ooh they get fat! The subjects. Do. They do! I am not fat I drink water.

*The **Page** pours another glass and hands it to him, but the **King** does not drink.*

Take Handel for an example. Greatest composer in the history of noise, but fat as a Christmas goose. Yuk! Hope I never for if I'm too gross the great ship of state will turn turtle damn my dung and I'm captain I'd drown last of all I'd be lonely in the freezing cold flood! Captain Cook, d'you see, has told me of the icebergs. My very worstest dream. The sea cluttered with icebergs . . .

He drops his glass in terror. It shatters on the floor.

Like the wreck of a shattered world.

I am the King of Icebergs. And the Ark has passed me by.

*A bell sounds, off. The **Page** manhandles the **King** roughly into a special chair with straps at wrists and ankles. The **King** is secured. The **Page** exits.*

Oh oh oh oh I am like sad Lear but thank God I have no Regan, no Goneril, only a clutch of Cordelias and the Prince of bloody Wales . . . and my Amelia, my Amelia, who's now a nest of worms, lucky old thing . . .

*The **Page** returns with a series of pills and evil-looking medicines which he proceeds to administer to the **King**, who shrieks his annoyance. He continues to speak during pauses in this 'treatment'.*

Sad stuff, Shakespeare, sorry stuff, he's missed the mark – for the thing about a King is that a King can do no wrong, he can't be judged naughty or guilty or bad nor prosecuted criminally in tort or in contract in any court in the land or the dominions beyond the blasted seas! Aaaargh!

Oh my dear babies, do not forsake me because the pendulum of my mind has come to rest. I am good. I am a good King. I've never even seen Hanover, that horrid Electorate which has always lived upon the very vitals of this poor country. I born *here*! I glory in the name of Briton! Heart of oak! Head of ash! Never wanted to rule without Parliament – just wanted to rule Parliament, damn and blast the disobedient dogs!

The 'treatment' ends. The **Page** *releases the* **King.**

Phew. Be calm. I have lived on the active theatre of this world some six hundred years a man of sorrow and acquainted with grief and if I am not wise enough to consider every event which happens quietly and with acquiescence I must have lived very negligently. Shut your eyes I will play for you. Hush now. I will play for those boneheads among ye, of whom we sometimes hear much, saying there be sick and rotten stuff at the root of this our happy nation. Those who I am told would tear down God, would set sail for a mighty turnabout dear oh dear. Would ye have a bloody republic here? And make all men equal? And women too? Ye would see the crowned heads of Europe fall from their scented necks and tumble in the gutters, hey? Would play kick-ball with the Lord's anointed brains? Damn me, sirs, madams, your republic comes damned close to my personal vision of hell. What? No God? No King? No lords? No servants? One ruthless law for all? We have never heard such ferocious stuff. We refute it, we confound it, we deny it from deep in the ruins of our being. Hang it all, I am the living proof the shattered relic survivor of the flood and bless us underwater hero of the nation's great advance. I continue to continue and here's my song.

He plays a great crashing discord on the harpsichord, and stops. The **Page** *stands next to him and sings directly into his ear, very beautifully indeed. It's 'See The Conquering Hero Comes' from Handel's 'Judas Maccabeus':*

Page
'See the conquering hero comes,
Sound the trumpets, beat the drums.
See the conquering hero comes,
Sound the trumpets, beat the drums.'

The **King** *is transfixed with delight.*

King There! There! Hear it! Conquering hero. That's me! England's glory! Pax Brittannicus! Me!

I know what I'll do. I know what I'll damn well do. I'll escape that's what I'll damn well do. I'll escape, and sit once more on my burnished throne! Find my Queen and my babies and rule the land again! Escape! Escape! Away flies the bat!

He runs round the room flapping his wings and biting the furniture, quite demented. He crashes into things, rips and tears at fabrics, cries and yelps. The **Page** *runs after him, trying to restrain him, but the* **King** *is possessed of great energy, and breaks away. At length the* **Page** *just trips him up. The* **King** *collapses on the floor and suffers a brief convulsive fit. The* **Page** *stands by, watching.*

(*Through chattering teeth.*) Ugh ugh . . . oh oh . . . fetch the leech . . . fetch the Royal Leech . . . quick! Ugh . . . ugh . . . fire in the blood . . . water on the brain . . . Haargh! (*He chokes.*) Fetch the five million physicians! Quick! I don't want . . . to die . . .

Slowly he subsides. Long pause. He lays still on the floor.

Oh I've wet meself.

Please help us up.

The **Page** *helps him get to his feet. He stands with as much dignity as he can muster.*

Our business is concluded I think Mr Ambassador and please let me be the first to apologise for the smell. You have read this Declaration of Impudence to me and although I hold that all men are not created equal and that they are not endowed by their Creator with any inalienable rights whatsoever still I have listened tolerantly with my inner ear, and have noted something brazen in your manner, which I suspect to be the herald of some brutish barren future. I harbour no doubts that when you return to your own country there will be some debate as to whether I am like I am due to some horrid disorder of the blood our dull physicians cannot diagnose, or whether I am like I am due to the cares of state having at some juncture become too heavy for my lightweight mind. I say does it matter, sir? I am still King of all I can see, Regency or no. And my descendants will themselves be in that happy position when next the question is put. Aye, 'tis a grand thing for a family man to think on, who has so many times sewn his oats in the royal fertiliser, and who can now rest assured that if he is like he is due to some foul humour in the blood, then by God all his offspring and all their offspring down all the leafy branches of the tree may suffer it as well which should give you something to consider on your way home. Hey, ho. Look to your Princesses. Their dark and gloomy side. And stand up straight when I'm talking to you. In my bleaker moments I do admit a doubt that this tainted line can survive down the centuries. Subjects'll never stand for it, I conclude. Dice of history roll against us. But damn my dingle will you look at the hullabaloo I have lived through? Eh? All the world in flames, but still the crumbly blood-pudding of our privilege bonds together, and we like the phoenix arise from the ashes of Old England! Hip hip! Huzza! Hip hip! Huzza!

He sits, exhausted. The **Page** *steps forward and tilts his chair slightly from behind.*

Now I must go to bed. And so this audience is hereby terminated. But I remain, Mr Ambassador, my Lords, Ladies, Gentlemen, and Others, His Majesty George the Third, by the grace of God, of Great Britain, Ireland, and the Dominions beyond the Seas, King, Defender of the Faith, nor your nor anybody's servant, and thoroughly deserving of blissful extinction. Proclamation for this day, eighteen hundred and something or other. Now I will let you go.

God save Me.

Very gently, the **Page** *takes the* **King**'s *hand and leads him off.*